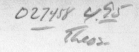
# THE UNKNOWABLE GURDJIEFF

Margaret Anderson first became known as the founder and editor of the *Little Review*, which between 1914 and 1929 published the work of many writers who were subsequently to become famous, including James Joyce, T. S. Eliot, Ezra Pound and Wyndham Lewis. The opening chapters of Joyce's *Ulysses* were first published in the *Little Review* until, in October 1920, the editors were arrested for publishing 'obscene literature'. It has been said that no American magazine has made so much literary history as the *Little Review* in those years. Margaret Anderson afterwards went to live in France and there came into contact with G. I. Gurdjieff. She died in 1973.

MARGARET ANDERSON

———————

# THE UNKNOWABLE GURDJIEFF

ARKANA

To Jane Heap, without whose illustrations I would have
understood less of Gurdjieff's doctrine of the 'Fourth Way'

ARKANA

Published by the Penguin Group
Penguin Books Ltd, 27 Wrights Lane, London w8 5tz, England
Viking Penguin, a division of Penguin Books USA Inc.
375 Hudson Street, New York, New York 10014, USA
Penguin Books Australia Ltd, Ringwood, Victoria, Australia
Penguin Books Canada Ltd, 2801 John Street, Markham, Ontario, Canada l3r 1b4
Penguin Books (NZ) Ltd, 182–190 Wairau Road, Auckland 10, New Zealand

Penguin Books Ltd, Registered Offices: Harmondsworth, Middlesex, England

First published in Great Britain by Routledge & Kegan Paul 1962
First published in the USA by Samuel Weiser, Inc. 1970
Published by Arkana 1991

5

Printed in England by Clays Ltd, St Ives plc

# CONTENTS

IN THE BEGINNING our special Gurdjieff group included:

A. R. ORAGE, former editor of the English *New Age*.

JANE HEAP ('jh'), co-editor of the *Little Review*.

GEORGETTE LEBLANC, singer, actress, author of *My Life with Maeterlinck* and *La Machine à Courage*.

SOLITA SOLANO, author of *Statue in a Field*.

Later on, KATHRYN HULME, author of *The Wild Place* and *The Nun's Story*.

And still later, MRS. ENRICO CARUSO, author of *Enrico Caruso: His Life and Death*, and *Dorothy Caruso: A Personal History*.

# I

# AN EVOCATION

ONE NIGHT last winter—one of those nights of cold unending rain that one never expects on the Riviera—I opened a book, *The Days Before*, by Katherine Anne Porter. I had been told that she had written about Katherine Mansfield, and I hoped she had understood Katherine's experience at the Gurdjieff Institute, about which so many distorted reports have been published.

Two or three years ago I had read Katherine's letters to Middleton Murry, and had been so moved by what she said of the months she spent with Gurdjieff at Fontainebleau that I felt I understood all she hadn't been able to say. Now I wanted to read what Katherine Anne Porter had to say about Katherine Mansfield's life, as well as her art.

On page 82 I came upon this sentence: 'She believed (or was persuaded that she believed) she could achieve a spiritual and mental rebirth by the

practice of certain disciplines and the study of esoteric doctrines.' On page 87 came the summing-up:
'She deliberately abandoned writing . . . She had
won her knowledge honestly, and she turned away
from what she knew to pursue some untenable
theory of personal salvation under a most dubious
teacher.'

I closed the book and listened to the relentless
rain. Katherine's miracle—('the laws of one cosmos
operating in another')—had been dismissed, denied, in a few irresponsible words.

It is now thirty-five years since a group of my
friends and I went to see Gurdjieff at the Château
du Prieuré in Fontainebleau-Avon, to ask if we
might study with him. From that day to this day
his thought and his science have shaped our lives. I
often try to imagine what life would have been
like without Gurdjieff. The first image that comes
to me is a simple one: it would be like trying to
imagine, from a prison window, what life is like
outside.

How distressing it is (and how unsurprising) to
discover, as I so often do, the number of intelligent
people to whom Gurdjieff is unknown and by
whom, in consequence, he is vilified.

For one, there is François Mauriac, that sympathetic Frenchman whose prose delights me,

whose nostalgic emotions so often meet my own,
but whose Catholicism leaves me in the same state
of rebellion and mystification as do all the other
organized religions of the world. Considering the
deformations that have permeated 'religion'
through the ages, it isn't astonishing to find that
Mauriac has decided to regard Gurdjieff as a char-
latan, or that he wrote not long ago:

[Katherine Mansfield savait] qu'il y a 'quelque chose
d'autre'. Nous la voyons un peu de temps rôder au tour
du catholicisme. C'est finalement au mage Gurdjieff
qu'elle donne sa foi—dans son phalanstère de Fontainebleau qu'elle vient s'abattre misèrablement. Ce qui l'y
avait poussée, c'était cette idée qu'il ne sert à rien de
soigner le corps, qu'il faut retrouver son âme afin de ne
pas mourir . . . Tant de souffrance aurait pu l'amener
ailleurs, vers une autre lumière. La petite fille perdue
s'est trompée de route. Mais elle a cherché, elle a aspiré.
C'est tout ce qui nous est demandé. Le reste relève de la
grâce.

(Katherine Mansfield knew there is 'something else'.
We see her for a little while considering the possibility
of Catholicism. In the end it was to Gurdjieff, the *mage*,
that she gave her faith, at the phalanstery of Fontainebleau, where she went to die in misery. What had led
her there was the belief that it is useless to nurse the
body, that one must regain one's soul in order not to
die . . . So much suffering could have led her elsewhere,
towards another enlightenment. The poor little girl lost

her way. But she aspired, she searched. That is all that is asked of us. The rest depends on grace).

There are, to me, at least five false judgments in this summary. Little by little I will show why I think so.

This kindly man, so open to all that is elevated, so indulgent towards much that is not, has been willing to condemn someone of whom he knows nothing at first hand; and to condemn him, in other critical articles, in extreme terms.

I wanted to write him a letter. But, knowing how he would answer—if he *did* answer, which was doubtful—I gave up the idea. Though I could have carried on a debate with him for months or years, if invited to, I decided that instead of writing a letter it would be better to write a book; and to write it as if it were a matter of life or death to me to convince Mauriac of his error.

Such a book would have to be written simply, clearly, and untechnically. Well, I can write simply, because I don't know any other way to write. And perhaps I can write clearly, because I believe in Gurdjieff. I believe in what he taught, and I believe it so intensely that, in spite of my limitations, surely *something* of his intention should shine through my conviction, even if it shines dimly.

Thus François Mauriac is in a way responsible for this book.

4

## An Evocation

It should of course be written by someone else—someone equipped to write it. But no one comes forward with the kind of book which I think could make Gurdjieff plain.

'*Can* he be made plain?'
'No. But some of his ideas can be made plain.'
'To whom?'
'I really don't know. But when I remember what pains he took to make plain some of his most difficult teaching, I think someone should try at least to make plain his function—what he called his "obligation".'
'Why?'
'So that there will be fewer people to whom one wants to cry, "Is it nothing to you, all ye who pass by?"'

Several books have been written about the Gurdjieff science. Ouspensky did his prodigious best, but his *In Search of the Miraculous* is difficult reading for those who approach it without first having had some contact with Gurdjieff. Orage did his expert best, only to be regarded by many as 'a slave to a fad', a 'doomed disciple of that weird mystic Gurdjieff'. Others have tried, but their efforts have been largely negated by their use of the Gurdjieff terminology, which is obscure unless first presented by Gurdjieff himself. His own book, *All and Everything*, is, I think, incomprehensible to anyone who hasn't studied with him. His *Meetings with Re-*

5

*markable Men*\* has already attracted five thousand readers in France, but only because its teaching is outweighed by its anecdotal interest.

The fact is that Gurdjieff remains unknown, except to those followers who worked with him.

One reason for this non-recognition is that it is too difficult to write about him. His science belongs to the knowledge of antiquity, and this knowledge is transmitted by word of mouth, never written about except in general terms.

Second, it is difficult to explain the difference between Gurdjieff's doctrine and the vaguer religious doctrines of the East. These philosophies and practises, based on the 'great truths', have taught men much, but they have not taught 'conscious knowledge' in Gurdjieff's way; nor (as I think can be proved) have they taught with his clarity and power.

But Gurdjieff is not only unknown. Perhaps he is unknowable.

A Gurdjieffan I know puts it this way: 'Gurdjieff's failure was that he produced no single disciple who understood what was wanted of him.'

Perhaps this is true. I suppose it must be, I suppose it is inevitable. But I wonder why I don't

\* *Rencontres avec des Hommes Remarquables* (Juillard).

quite believe it; why I think it is close to, but not totally, the truth.

'If what you say is true,' I argue, 'why do the Gurdjieff groups continue their efforts today? Why did Gurdjieff make his effort? We can't believe that he was without foreknowledge of his failure (if such it was). Why then did he work with pupils? More for his own sake than for theirs?'

'In a way. The pupils are as necessary to the teacher as the teacher to the pupils; the teacher is obliged to give back what he has received. But Gurdjieff never found a man who was able to raise himself to "the step below the master". Yet thousands, due to Gurdjieff, took one, even two, steps up that stairway of the "Fourth Way", and their lives were vitalized and purified, even with a minimum of work.'

This I *know* to be true. So instead of saying that no disciple understood what was wanted of him, I would say that several may have understood but that they found it too difficult to do what was wanted.

The only thing one KNOWS is that if Gurdjieff's theory of human evolution were understood and practised, our planet would be freed of hate, madness and war. But since these states are, apparently, the conditions through which men are destined to struggle, it seems superfluous to try to change them.

The conclusion therefore would appear to be that nothing can be done, that nothing should even be attempted, to release humanity from its sad, savage, repetitive fate.

These were my negative musings on that winter night.

Since they weren't conducive to sleep, and since a negative attitude isn't natural to me, I kept on thinking until I came to an idea.

If one has the extravagant ambition to create an awareness of Gurdjieff's function and accomplishment, one must choose a responsive audience. Why not ignore the genus intellectual, since it is usually the last to respond with great emotion to a great idea, and address oneself to the kind of people who, Gurdjieff said, wanted and could benefit by what he had to offer. He described them as people who possess a 'magnetic centre'—that is, those who have a place in themselves which can receive the substance of great knowledge, those who are susceptible to the influence of 'higher forces'. He divided such people into two groups—the first composed of those in whom 'education' has not atrophied the tendency of aspiration; the second, of those he called 'simple man'.

This elimination of 'the many' would mean accepting Gurdjieff's dictum that only small numbers of men can develop those 'quality vibrations' which can change their fate; that they in turn can influence others who are influencable; and that thus the 'accident' into which all men are born has, sometimes, a happy turning.

My conception of an understandable book about Gurdjieff is that it should be addressed to the two types of influencable aspirants, and written as far as possible (at least in the beginning) in words of one syllable.

I would pass over facts (biographical) and concentrate on teaching. I have little interest in the facts that people seem to want most . . . where was he born? what were his circumstances? his education? his training? what legends grew up about him? was he the precepteur of the Dalai Lama? etc., etc., etc. Gurdjieff himself has written about his childhood, his parents, his teachers, his travels, his experiences, his knowledge. What matters is the knowledge.

In this book I shall write of what he said when I was there to hear him say it; of what he taught us, how he taught it, and what effect it had not only upon me but upon my friends, since each of us experienced it differently, and each of us has written of it in her own way.

Such a book is far from being a study, a portrait,

a treatise, a manual or a document. I should like it
to be a sort of primer. The most I hope to accomplish is an evocation; the least, a rectification—
which will prevent anyone from ever again having the hardihood to call Gurdjieff an imposter.

I would call this accomplishing a great deal.

## II

# SUPER-KNOWLEDGE

THOUGH GURDJIEFF may have left no heir, I
know at least three 'disciples' who are com-
petent to convey the essence of what may
be called his super-knowledge. There may be
others. . . .

Of the three I know, one was entrusted by Gurdjieff to carry on his work in France. Ever since his
death she has done what is too difficult to do.

One day she and I were talking about the too-
difficult, and I asked her what she thought *I* could
do that would be useful. I had already had the idea
of a book—'But how', I asked her, 'dare I try to
write about Gurdjieff when I haven't the brain to
do it?'

'You're *for* him, not *against* him, aren't you?'

Such simplicity staggered me. I could only say,
'As you so well know.'

'Then try,' she said.

So I am trying.

For a long time I debated with myself about an effective way to introduce Gurdjieff to anyone who approaches him with antagonism. I kept on saying, 'I can't do it, I don't know enough.' For instance, there are scientific charts and diagrams which exemplify his ideas but which I can't understand, and couldn't understand even if my incapacity were threatened with torture. But this is because I am allergic to charts. I can never, for example, find my way through a city if someone makes me a diagram to follow. I ask him to direct me verbally, then I can arrive. When I was taught to drive a car, it took me much longer than necessary because my teacher refused to teach me in the only way I can learn—by simply answering in sequence any questions I needed to ask. If anyone would answer my step-by-step questions about the Gurdjieff charts, I think I could finally understand them; but I have never found such a person, either in or outside the Gurdjieff groups. Like Henry James, who remained a stranger to arithmetic, I must remain oblivious to charts as a guide to the Gurdjieff 'system'. Oh, I have studied and memorized them, and I have a general idea of their meaning; but really to understand and explain them is something else. I can play chess, I understand the significance and power of each piece, I can even win; but I wouldn't feel

I *understood* the game unless I had invented it.

There are other aspects of Gurdjieff's teaching that I know I do understand, and that I can explain. Besides, it isn't a question of knowing *everything*, but of understanding *something*. I have only to select, or quote, from all that I found wonderful.

Remembering the injunction that 'You must give to others, you have to learn not only to understand but to explain; and you will see that *you can understand certain things only by explaining them to others*' . . . I thought: what good am I doing in the world if I don't make this effort? how else can I 'repay' my debt for having been born to a life on earth, and 'repay' Gurdjieff for teaching me how I could live that life more consciously?

I decided that I could use his own words as an introduction to his ideas.

But first, it would have to be understood that these ideas cannot be made available to everyone. The masses don't want them, and couldn't understand them. Clergymen, priests, evangelists, Billy Grahams, serve the needs of those whose aspirations and capacities are on a different level, and who, in the hierarchy of 'accident', never rise above that level.

Second, this arbitrary classification would have to be justified, and Gurdjieff himself has done it:*

*In Search of the Miraculous*, by P. D. Ouspensky. (London, 1950).

# Super-Knowledge

*Question:* Why, if ancient knowledge has been preserved and if there has always existed a knowledge distinct from our science and philosophy, or even surpassing it, is it so carefully concealed? Why are the men who possess this special knowledge unwilling to let it pass into general circulation, for the sake of a better and more successful struggle with deceit, ignorance and evil?

*Gurdjieff:* There are two answers. In the first place, this knowledge is not concealed; and in the second place it cannot, from its very nature, become common property.

I will prove to you that *knowledge* is far more accessible to those capable of assimilating it than is generally supposed; and that the whole trouble is that people either do not want it or cannot receive it.

But first of all another thing must be understood, namely, that knowledge cannot belong to all, cannot even belong to many. Such is the law. You do not understand this because you do not understand that knowledge, like everything else in the world, is material. This means that it possesses all the characteristics of materiality. One of the first characteristics of materiality is that matter in a given place and under given conditions is limited. . . . The matter of knowledge possesses entirely different qualities according to whether it is taken in small or large quantities. Taken in a large quantity in a given place, that is, by one man, or by a small group of men, it produces very good results; taken in a small quantity (that is, by everyone of a large number of people) it gives no results at all; or it may even give negative results, contrary to those expected. Thus, if a certain definite quantity of knowledge is distributed among millions of people, each individual will receive very little, and this small amount of knowledge will change nothing either in his life or in his understanding of things.

But if, on the contrary, large quantities of knowledge are concentrated in a small number of people, then knowledge will give very good results.

At the first glance this theory seems very unjust, since the position of those who are, so to speak, denied knowledge in order that others may receive a greater share, appears to be very sad and undeservedly harder than it ought to be. Actually, however, this is not so at all; and in the distribution of knowledge there is not the slightest injustice.

The fact is that the majority of people do not want any knowledge whatever; they refuse their share of it, and do not even take the ration allotted to them in the general distribution for the purposes of life. This is particularly evident in times of mass madness such as wars, revolutions . . . when men seem to lose even the small amount of common sense they had and turn into complete automatons, giving themselves over to wholesale destruction in vast numbers . . . even losing the instinct of self-preservation. Owing to this, enormous quantities of knowledge remain unclaimed and can be distributed among those who realize its value.

There is nothing unjust in this, because those who receive knowledge take nothing that belongs to others; they take only what others have rejected as useless and what in any case would be lost if they did not take it.

The collection of knowledge by some depends upon the rejection of knowledge by others.

The other aspect consists in the fact that no one is concealing anything; there is no mystery whatever. But the acquisition or transmission of true knowledge demands great labour and great effort from him who receives and from him who gives. And those who possess this knowledge are doing everything they can to transmit it to the greatest number of people, to facilitate people's approach to it and enable them to prepare themselves to receive the truth. But knowledge cannot be given by force to anyone, and an unprejudiced survey of the average man's life, of what fills his day, and of the things he is interested in, will at once show whether it is possible to accuse men who possess knowledge of concealing it, of not wishing to teach people what they know themselves.

. . . Knowledge cannot come to people without effort on their own part. People understand this very well in connexion with ordinary knowledge, but in the case of *great knowledge*, when they admit the possibility of its existence, they find it possible to expect something different. Everyone knows that if a man wants to learn Chinese it will take several years of intense work; everyone knows that five years are needed to grasp the principles of medicine, and perhaps twice as many years for the study of painting or music. And yet there are theories which affirm that knowledge can come to people without any effort on their part. The very existence of such theories constitutes an additional explanation of why knowledge cannot *come* to people.

At the same time it is essential to understand that man's *independent* effort to attain anything in this direction can also give no results. A man can only attain knowledge with the help of those who possess it.

*One must learn from one who knows.*


When you went to Gurdjieff to study, only one demand was made upon you—that you *work*. You weren't asked to try to change your nature, or give up your business, or 'enter a monastery', but seriously to apply yourself to acquiring the three-dimensional life Gurdjieff's knowledge could prepare you for. The 'work' had to take first place in your scheme or nothing would be accomplished. This was the great difficulty in the beginning.

When I first heard of this concentration on a paramount aim, I thought of a pianist friend of mine, Carol Robinson, who spends several weeks a year teaching in one of the large American colleges for girls. The first thing she always says to a new group is, 'You must understand that if any of you were really going to become pianists you wouldn't be here.'

It was a similar preoccupation with a single aim that was my chief problem year after year with Gurdjieff (as it is with everyone, I'm sure). I re-

member when I was trying to write *The Fiery
Fountains* and decided that I must stop going to him
every day; I couldn't write a book and study intensely with him at the same time—I was sacrificing
the book by this division of energies, and I wanted
to finish it because it might make some money
which we badly needed.

One day I told Gurdjieff that I wouldn't be coming to him every day for a while.

'Why?' he asked.

'Because I must finish my book.'

'Book is nothing,' he said. 'If not come to me
now, perhaps later will be too late to come. Then
cannot come any more than you can kiss your own
elbow.'

So I decided to renounce the book and go back
to the daily hours of effort in his terms. And, as
always when you have made a right decision, the
'fates' conspired to help me. Gurdjieff soon left for
America and I had three free months before me in
which to finish the book.

In one part of it I described the struggle I had
gone through for years in trying to incorporate his
knowledge. I called this part 'A Life for a Life'.

Much later, when the book was published (after
I had returned to America during the war), I asked
a neighbour—a simple, serious person—if she had
been interested in what I wrote about Gurdjieff.

'I was interested, yes,' she said, 'but it was all beyond me. How could you expect me to understand it? I'm just a housewife, and a mother. I have a husband and two children whom I love and for whom I want the best. Gurdjieff gave *you* something, I could see that; but what could he give me and my family?'

It was a difficult question, to which I had too many answers. And what a long time it would have taken to answer briefly. Besides, could I have made any of it clear?

Then one day our neighbour asked Dorothy,* 'What is it you have that gives me the feeling of a great serenity? I wish I knew, and that I could have it too.'

As always, Dorothy answered in simple words which somehow managed to convey something of the essence of Gurdjieff's theories. She used none of his terminology but spoke in the most easy human way.

'Oh,' said our neighbour, 'how wonderful! How can I find out more about it?'

When people ask, 'Do I have to read an incomprehensible book like Gurdjieff's *All and Everything*?', I am reminded of Thornton Wilder's answer to a woman who asked him whether she

* Mrs. Enrico Caruso.

ought to read Joyce's *Ulysses* and *Finnegan's Wake*.

'I'm just a housewife,' she said. 'I have three children. I belong to the P.T.A. Do I have to read books like these?'

Wilder said: 'Did you ever read Rousseau's *Emile* or *La Nouvelle Héloise*? I never did—but I can pretty well believe that all of us, whether we know it or not, have been in large part formed by them. Every century has its underground books which have permeated thought. Often they have been transmitted through relatively few readers. I believe those two great books of Rousseau are shaping us still—though many of us will never read them.'

I can think of another way to introduce the Gurdjieff 'theory': by comparing it with other theories that are prevalent today.

Many people are now reading and discussing the philosophy of Zen. But to us, Dr. Suzuki—the interpreter of Zen Buddhism, with a large following in the western world—is a teacher to whom we could never have turned.

We had already had enough of terminologies like this: 'The finite is infinite . . . *Prajna* lays its hands on Emptiness, or Suchness, or Self-Nature . . . the grasping must be no-grasping, accomplished by nondiscrimination, that is by nondiscriminating discrimination,' etc. No, no, if Gurdjieff had offered this kind of thing we would never have sought him out.

But there is a small book by Eugen Herrigel, *Zen in the Art of Archery*, which parallels in a striking way the method of Gurdjieff's teaching, and which to all of us, I think, constitutes the only psychological event we have encountered since the advent of Gurdjieff in our lives. I also think it is doubtful that anyone can understand—really understand—this book unless he has first listened to Gurdjieff (I have read several attempts at interpretation). All that Herregel discloses about his six years of instruction in archery might serve as a manual of Gurdjieff's daily psychological instruction, and might help people to understand why this super-psychology begins where all our orthodox psychology ends.

Another way to begin talking about Gurdjieff might be this:

Man is born into the captivity of Nature, with his super-natural part passive and hidden from him. With the greatest degree of natural intelligence he can never find anything in himself but mind, feeling, and senses. Only with assistance, instruction and *revelation* added to faith, the *fire* of wish and undeviating purpose, can he succeed in being 'born again'.

For 'rebirth' there is an exact science, the greatest in the world.

Not long ago I decided to read Sartre's *Being and Nothingness*. I had always been willing to imagine that there must be *something* in existentialism, but uninterested in investigating it, knowing that it would be nothing in comparison with the Gurdjieff super-knowledge.

I read on and on—discovering, indeed, 'nothingness': 'A freedom which wills itself freedom is in fact a being-which-is-not-what-it-is and which-is-what-it-is-not, and which chooses as the ideal of being, being-what-it-is-not and not-being-what-it-is.' Or this: 'The possible is a structure of the for-itself. Being-in-itself is never either possible or impossible. Being is. Being is in-itself. Being is what it is.'

Doubtless! . . . if you don't recognize such 'titillation' for what *it* is: simply a new Tower of Babel—of all approaches to Being one of the most certain to lead nowhere. Such a book is the summit of what Gurdjieff called 'philosophysing'—'pouring from the empty into the void'. ('Only a philosopher can understand other philosophers,' he said. 'Children and animals alone have the property of pure magicality. They do not philosophize'.)

What does Sartre reveal about 'knowing himself'? about knowing anyone else? about knowing anything that must be known if one starts on a quest of that exact science which says that a man must be born again?

But I am forgetting Gurdjieff's primary premise that should be stated first of all in the pursuit of self-knowledge:

'Man is a biological product of three inter-acting centres—physical, emotional, mental. We are in a state of arrested development because our mental and emotional centres are not developed.'

Since this book is not a treatise, but an intimation, I will quote at random certain formulations of the Gurdjieff cosmology that give a kind of orchestration of his thinking:

The universe is an intelligent scheme (plan, idea), and is therefore intelligible. The Gurdjieff ideas are a pattern of thinking—a great thinking-machine. Any question the mind of man can put has been answered. At the base of things there is not just a mystery. The nature of things lie together in harmony. The real world is the evolution of an idea.

Man's obligation is to co-operate with the laws which operate the universe. The realization of the working of certain laws is the kingdom of heaven.

The obligation goes with the fact that man has a unique place. But the awareness of his place is not a gift of nature. No man by *wishing*, or by *taking thought*, can do anything about his development. He must do something unique. This method offers this unique activity.

Since we have no technique for development, our life is like a dream. In dreams we don't choose or invent events. Our life is like that. And we can't voluntarily wake from this dream. We wake, or develop, only if the dream becomes unbearable, or if someone shakes us awake.

The octave was originally a formula to explain cosmic truths—only later was it used musically.

The octave is a mathematical formula, in respect of sound, through which all creation (physical and psychical) must pass, upward and downward, in the phenomenal changes of nature.

A state of consciousness has a place (relative position) in the cosmos. The Sermon on the Mount—a high state of consciousness.

By conscious thoughts, emotions, acts, we feed ourselves. God, when He made the universe, made self-feeding.

Time is only the exhaustion of the means to renew ourselves.

Knowledge and Understanding are quite different. Only Understanding can lead to Being, whereas Knowledge is only a passing presence in it. One must *strive* to understand. This alone can lead to our Lord God, and in order to understand the phenomena of Nature according to Law, one must first of all consciously perceive and assimilate a mass of information concerning objective truth and the events which really took place on earth in the past; and secondly, one must be the bearer of all kinds of personal-experiences-personally-experienced.

Perhaps one of my own experiences, after several years of working with Gurdjieff, may be *à propos*.

It was a kind of vision—the sort of illuminated 'seeing' that happens with great suddenness, lasts for an instant, and leaves an indelible impression. Such moments are rare, and usually happen when you have been making great effort or have been harassed beyond endurance, too discouraged to go on trying at all.

One morning, after a night of anguish, I sat up in bed as if I had been catapulted from sleep. I had had, in a flash, an answer to the recurring question: 'Why do we work with Gurdjieff? Why do we do the "exercises" (physical, emotional, mental) he gives? What are they really for?'

The answer traced back to a statement of his—a statement he never ceased to repeat and which was, to most people, the most antagonistic of all his pronouncements: 'Man has no soul; he has only the potentiality.'

We have always assumed that man is born with a soul, that this is the endowment which distinguishes him from animals. But now in my vision I saw that you can't say a man is born with a soul any more than you can say that he is born with an art. A man may be born an artist—that is, with an art tendency—but he won't have an art until he has worked at art, developed it through an organic process of growth. He must live a life of Art. In the same way, a man can't have a soul until he has lived a life of the Soul.

So I began to understand at last—after how many years?—the reason for the Gurdjieff 'exercises': you work with them to make the soul function just as a painter works with colour and design to make his painting function. This 'great discovery' seems so simple that you can't imagine why you haven't always known it, especially since it has been suggested to you from the beginning. But when it strikes you as a piece of original thinking—as it struck me that long-ago morning—it's as if you had solved the whole mystery of the world.

I have always been moved by Eliphas Levi's words about men like Gurdjieff:

What secret do these men bear with them to the tomb? Why are they wondered at without being understood?

Why are they acquainted with things of which others know nothing? Why do they conceal what all men burn to know?

There is indeed a formidable secret. . . . There is a science and a force. . . . There is one sole, universal and imperishable doctrine, strong as the supreme reason, simple like all that is great, intelligible like all that is universally and absolutely true. This doctrine has been the parent of all others . . . . The secret constitutes the science of 'good' and 'evil', and the secret of indefinite human progress is in that expression 'the Kingdom of Heaven'.

# III

# TRANSFORMATION

EVERYONE WHO went to Gurdjieff for enlightenment encountered, first, a mystery. I have
always found Solita Solano's account of her
first meetings with him interesting touching, and
amusing. She is one of the persons whose life has
been changed by what she learned from him.

It was in 1927 that I first met Mr. Gurdjieff. Margaret
Anderson and Jane Heap had invited me to go with them
to the Prieuré at Fontainebleau, saying, 'There you will
see not one man, but a million men in one'. The magnitude of this interger excited me. I hoped for a demigod,
a superman of saintly countenance, not this 'strange'
écru man about whom I could see nothing extraordinary
except the size and power of his eyes. The impact everyone expected him to make upon me did not arrive. In
the evening I listened to a reading from his vaunted
book. It bored me. Thereupon I rejected him intellectually, although with good humour. Later in the study-
house (how annoyed I was that women were not allowed

to smoke there) I heard the famous music, played, I
believe, by Monsieur de Hartmann. This, almost from
the first measures, I also rejected. A week or so later in
Paris I accompanied Margaret and Jane, who had not
quite given me up, to a restaurant where *écrivisses* were
the speciality which Mr. Gurdjieff was coming to eat
with about twenty of his followers. He seated me next
to him and for two hours muttered in broken English.
I rejected his language, the suit he was wearing and his
table manners; I decided that I rather disliked him.

Years passed.

In the autumn of 1934, in a crisis of misery, I suddenly
knew that I had long been waiting to go to him and that
he was expecting me. I sought him out and sat before
him, silent. . . . He was then living in the Grand Hotel,
over the Café de la Paix—his 'office', while waiting for
a flat to be found. The Prieuré group had dispersed,
there were no followers or pupils near him except Eliza-
beth Gordon who sometimes came to the Café. Three
friends of mine, who had previously met Mr. Gurdjieff,
also began to go to the Café to see him. Within a few
days he gave us chapters of 'Beelzebub' to read aloud to
him. And thus, by such an 'accident', we four formed
the nucleus of a new group which was to grow larger
year by year until the end of his life.

After Gurdjieff's death many people asked us
how they could learn more about him. 'It's hard to
know where to start,' they said. 'There are so many
Gurdjieff groups now, and so many teachers who

haven't time for new pupils; and then I often get the impression that there's a kind of intellectual snobbery about the whole thing, and this puts me off.'

We too often had the same impression. Besides, it was impossible for us, who 'had had so many years of first-hand contact with Gurdjieff himself, to join any of the new miscellaneous groups. Once Solita felt it a duty to try, and wrote me her reaction:

There were so many poor young strugglers, and so much nonsense in their questions and comments, that it was depressing. There was one young man, a rather new one, who made the only intelligent remark. 'It seems to me', he said, 'that the only difference between this and all other groups of religious or philosophical tendencies is the WORK.'

All these people, nearly all, are so staunch in devotion and loyalty that one has to love them for it. But there isn't one of sufficient intelligence to pierce those devotional veils—no mind like or in the same *gamme* as Ouspensky's. They don't combine mental and emotional, put them to work at the same moment—so will grow gooder and gooder without understanding anything transformational.

'Transformational' was the key word, and it meant an effort to strip off the mask of your personality so that your essence could develop—'personality' being your false picture of yourself, your 'emotional attitude towards yourself'. This stripping operation often presents itself to me now in images. The most frequent one is that I am carrying with me, wherever I go, a huge sack. In it is my personality—that manifesting 'animal' which expressed itself so incessantly for so many years, and that now lies dormant in the sack, stirring only faintly from time to time in its likes, dislikes, pleasures, rebellions, happinesses, angers and obsessions.

Gurdjieff's teaching on transformation was sometimes given like this:

There is an old Russian saying: 'A hunchback can be straightened only in the tomb'. Just so, a man must die to become changed.

I wish you not to be Nonentity. So first I make you feel like nonentity. Only from there can you begin.

It is nothing to *know* your nonentityness, you must experience it personally.

To know mentally is nothing, worth nothing. You must have a third kind of knowledge.

There is a passage in Gurdjieff's book which suggests the kind of knowledge he meant. Its title is 'The Sheep and the Wolf':

Only he will deserve the name of man and can count on anything prepared for him from Above who has already acquired corresponding data for the ability to preserve intact both the wolf and the sheep confided to his care. An old saying of ancient times definitely showed that by the word 'wolf' is allegorically understood the totality of all fundamental reflex-functioning of the human organism; and that by the word 'sheep' is understood the totality of a man's feeling. As for the functioning of a man's mentation, it is represented, according to the saying, by the man himself who in the process of his responsible life, owing to his Conscious Labours and Voluntary Sufferings, has acquired in his common presence corresponding data for the aforesaid ability always to create conditions for the possible existence together of these two heterogeneous and mutually alien animals (laws).

In every man there must be the constant striving that the wolf be full and the sheep intact.

For the 'wolf' I quote the first of the Five Obligations Gurdjieff gave us:

THE FIVE OBLIGATIONS (five strivings for daily effort)

1. *Preserve your life.* (Be just to the body; satisfy its needs; treat it as a good master treats a good servant.)

. . . and for the 'sheep', the other four:

2. *Find your place in the scheme.* (Understand the meaning and aim of existence. Know more and more concerning the laws of world creation and world maintenance.)

3. *Develop yourself.* (Constant, unflagging need for self-perfection in the sense of Being. Improve your 'being' make 'being' efforts.)

4. *Help others to develop.* (Assist in the most rapid perfectioning of other beings.)

5. *Pay back.* (To lighten the load of the Creator, pay back in gratitude and effort for the fact that Evolution has helped you to get this far.)

One day, years ago, a group of those whom Gurdjieff called 'his people' was lunching with him in New York. Afterwards one of the group* typed a report of the table conversation—a report which, because of her prodigious memory, is as factual as if it had been recorded on tape. I will quote it as she wrote it, in the Gurdjieff idiom. The language barrier gives an extra dimension, and the teaching contained in the conversation is typical of Gurdjieff's exposition:

K. attempts to clarify to Sapenshko something Gurdjieff has said. Sapenshko resents this, but with good nature; only his sudden earnestness betrays his offence. Sapenshko tells K. that only Gurdjieff can say such thing to him—'Not you, you are small man. But he—he can say anything to me and I can take. You know why? Because I love him.'

Gurdjieff waits until all is said, then turns to K. and in

* Kathryn Hulme.

quite another tone and with serious gentle look on his face, he begins:

'Truth, K., one fault you have. Though you are known as kind man, good nature, and though everyone knows you not wish give offence, you do this unconsciously sometimes. Is fault that spoils all life for you. You have not *considerateness for state of surroundings*. Necessary always know what is around you—state of man around you. With cow, you can spit on face of and he not take offence. He lick, he smile, he shake head; not understand, not offence take. But man around you is already more high—he have *states*. You must know what is state of every man around you in room. Man of course is most of time asleep, but this make even more important that you be sensitive . . . because when he awake, even if only for one moment, he is already in state—for this moment is delicate, sensitive. . . . So you must consciously try understand, be sensitive for him. I know what is state of each man around me because I am educated man, I have knowledge. You must always try have considerateness for state of surrounding if you wish be objective *bon-ton*.

'Never must you offend one thing on earth. Even if you offend one worm—one day . . . one day . . . he will you repay.

'You notice never anyone take offence anything I say?—never man angry with me when *I* tell? You know why? Because I tell *exact* how is, objective truth.'

On another day—in 1936, I think—we were all

lunching with Gurdjieff in his Paris flat. I had been feeling hopeless about ever being strong enough to do the inner work he demanded.

He had asked one of the pupils to give up smoking for a while and to turn her longing for a cigarette into what he called an 'intentional contact' between the ordinary world and a higher world. I felt that his words were especially offered to meet my need, and I quote them—with slight paraphrasings to make his meaning clear:

'I will tell you one thing that will make you rich for life.

'There are two struggles—an Inner-world struggle and an Outer-world struggle. But these two worlds can never make contact with each other, to make data for Third World; even God cannot give the possibility for contact between Inner-world and Outer-world struggle; neither can your heredity give it.

'Only *one* thing can give it: you must make an *intentional contact* between the two worlds; then you can make data which crystallize for the Third World of man, called by the ancients the World of the Soul.

'I can give you a small example which will perhaps give you the "taste" of this intentional contact. You, for example, when you give up cigarettes. You have an Outer-world struggle (not to buy, not to take, but remember always to break habit); and you have an Inner-world struggle (you imagine how it was when you could smoke—you imagine it in a different way, more keen, and with more longing); and it will seem (with this Inner-world imagining) even more desirable than it had ever been. You will have made this cigarette an Intentional Contact between the two struggles, and even by this small effort you will have made data for the Third World.

'This can be a thing for power. I will tell you one very important thing to say, each time when the longing to smoke comes. You say it the first time, and maybe notice nothing. You say it a second time, and maybe nothing. Say it a third time, and perhaps something will happen. Say: "I wish the result of this suffering to become my own, for Being". Yes, you can call that kind of wishing suffering, because it *is* suffering.

'This saying can maybe *take force from your animal* and give it to Being. And you can do this for many things— for any denial of something that is a *slavery*. A force such as this has special results, special emanations.

'Man is man—he can never be another thing. But he can make his body work for another part of him—his mind. If it is easy to subdue the body, then the exercise is no good. If the body will lie down at once, nothing happens. The greater weakness the body has, the more it is forced to struggle, the more labour it does, the more it can give to the mind, and to Being.'

Oh yes, say the Christians, this is exactly what we do. We resist temptation, we renounce, we become better human beings.

This is not true.

It is true that they often do renounce, or try to renounce, or think they have renounced. Then they forget that they have renounced, they feel remorseful, and they begin all over again to renounce. In every case they remain exactly the same kind of people they were in the beginning. The only results they achieve are that, at intervals, they behave more kindly towards other people; or they become more intolerant and cruel towards them (the stake for dissenters).

Some people become fanatical renouncers. And, since the exercise of will (so-called) produces strength in anyone, they sometimes become very strong people—strong enough to make a great impact upon others; strong enough to kill them.

All this will and effort is haphazard, none of it has any relation to a *conscious* self-directed activity for a *conscious* aim. The Gurdjieff technique for this development is a unique activity, and it has not been presented in any literature, science or teaching in the way it was presented by him.

The great science of transformation—the birth of the soul, that conscious 'second birth' which parallels automatic (physical) birth and for which Gurdjieff had such a marvellous phrase: 'the arising of the presence of man' . . . this transformation demands years of study and practice for its incorporation. 'Past joys', he said, 'are as useless to man in the present as the snows of last year which leave no trace by which one can remember what they were. Only the imprints of conscious labour and intentional suffering are Real, and can be used for obtaining good.'

This good comes to you step by step, in great 'discoveries'—for instance, like the one that teaches you why anger is so often an expression of self-love. I shall never forget the day when I first 'learned' this truth. I had spent a week of frenzied anger and rebellion over everything Gurdjieff was asking me to do. The conscious labour was too difficult, the voluntary suffering too unendurable, too impossible, too unreasonable. And then, in one lighted moment, I had a picture of myself, my state, and its cause. I rushed to the rue des Colonels Renard and said, 'Mr. Gurdjieff, I see now that it was because of my vanity and self-love that I was so angry.'

He didn't speak for a moment, then he smiled at me. 'You not know?' he said.

'No,' I said, 'I hadn't the faintest idea.'

Never, never, shall I forget the way he smiled, or the intonation he put into those three words. Never shall I fail to remember them as I watch myself making other discoveries that will take me as long a time; and never shall I fail to find comfort in six other words of his: 'He who goes slow goes far.'

One of my longest struggles was over my need to argue.

I have always been an arguer. I long to be convinced, and I can be convinced only if I receive rational answers to my questions. But this tendency was discouraged from the beginning.

'Asperity, impatience, tendency to argue,' I was told, 'at once put an end to any possibility of "work", for "work" is possible only as long as people remember they have come to the teacher to learn and not to teach. A certain vehemence is characteristic of the arguing type; he becomes unnecessary to the teacher. No feeding exchange is possible between teacher and pupil if the pupil refuses food and the teacher can't get to *his* larder. And the recalcitrant pupil spoils the atmosphere for others.'

'But why?' I kept asking. 'One of the first things I heard was "Be sceptical, don't take anything you hear on faith, investigate until you find out whether you can believe it". How can you investigate if you don't *reason*? And how can you reason if you don't ask questions, state objections, discuss, receive answers?'

'No,' I was admonished. 'When the thinking centre is always fighting something, disputing, criticizing, the reason is that it is using the energy of another centre. Gurdjieff wished to work only with those who could be useful to him in attaining his aim; and only those who would *struggle with themselves* could be useful to him. I take it that the refined vibrations obtained from *struggle* were the caviar he needed for his own food.'

'So I must struggle not to argue? But I can't have faith in anything unless I'm convinced, by discussion, of its truth. All that you say constitutes a paradox.'

'Paradox is present in all great truths.'

When you have finally grasped the meaning of transformation and realized how false your picture of yourself has been, when you have discovered the kind of person you really are, and heard (as Maurice Nicoll says) the little song you've been singing all your life . . . this is the moment when you can say that you've begun at the beginning. You will never be entirely your old self again—that is, you will know forever that that is what you were, and are, and will be over and over, but with this difference: the hair's-breadth difference that you now *know* it, and can never forget it, and therefore you will stop short of feeling, or showing, the intolerance you have always felt; you will begin to behave towards others as you would like them to behave towards you—the difference being that you will now *know* how they want you to behave, and you will know how to help them to behave well towards you. You will see that you are they and they are you, and that if everyone could experience this searing revelation the idea of war would never have arisen.

Paul Claudel once said in a radio interview, 'I don't hold with the doctrine of "Know thyself". I advise you to "forget yourself"—the world will be a better place.'

What an idea! How can you forget what you don't know? And how can ignorance be regarded as a proper foundation for an evolving humanity? But the great religionists will always prefer 'Forget yourself' to Gurdjieff's 'Re-member yourself'; will in fact look upon his injunction as somehow monstrous.

# IV

# THE UNKNOWN DOCTRINE

'WHY DIDN'T you tell me that the source of the Gurdjieff doctrine traces back to the Gnostics?'

'I forgot to,' I said.

I forgot because such a fact didn't particularly interest me—Gurdjieff himself was a sufficient source for me. All that he said was so vast that it left me no time to inquire about the original source. The knowledge he knew, wherever it came from, was far more important to me than any inquiries about its historical beginnings.

In Gurdjieff's own words, this knowledge traces back to 'initiate people'. Or, in another's words: 'The Gnostics were not the inventors of this ancient knowledge, any more than Gurdjieff was. All "cults", religions, teachers, go to this common "initiate source" or pool or storage-place and take from it whatever they are able. Then of course they falsify, until nothing is left of the original truths and their vitality. (I mean by "common source", available to all who are able to take from it.)'

There is another question which I am often asked, and which interests me far more than any discussion of sources. 'What are the things you first heard that convinced you of the value of Gurdjieff's doctrine?'

The very first?: Orage's presentation of that doctrine in a series of formulations that clarified, and corrected, what we had already vaguely heard of it in Ouspensky's *Tertium Organum*.

In the winter of 1924, in New York, we listened to Orage's oracular talk. We were hearing for the first time ideas of a kind we had never heard before. Then Gurdjieff himself came, presented a group of French pupils in his sacred 'dances', and talked to a large group of American intellectuals, with Orage translating.

In the spring we went to Fontainebleau, and there—under Gurdjieff's penetrating eye, as he weighed our capacities of 'attention, impressionability, alertness, intensity and sincerity'—we listened to chapters of *Beelzebub's Tales to His Grandson* read aloud. We began to work on the dance 'exercises', and we lived the daily life of the Prieuré—much as Katherine Mansfield has described it in her letters.

All this was sufficiently rewarding, but underneath everything that went on at the Prieuré there was for me, and for two others, a decisive influence. The two others were Jane Heap and Georgette Leblanc; and the decisive influence was the Orage mind. For myself I know that, without Orage's grasp of the Gurdjieff ideas, and his manner of elucidation, I might never have understood enough of them to have investigated further. I can think of no other approach that would completely have held my attention. (Gurdjieff's way of teaching—I should say his various ways of teaching—resembled nothing I had ever known or heard of, and were almost impossible for me to understand at first. It was only later that I realized why he taught as he did, instead of the way I wished he would!)

The fact is that for a long, long time I was completely baffled by Gurdjieff. But, because of the foundation laid during my first year, it would have taken more than bafflement to have turned me away.

Many years later, believing that there must be other people who would react as I did, I made a series of résumés of all the material that had most impressed me in the beginning. Organizing it into categories, I quoted from Orage, largely from Jane, and sometimes from simple re-formulations of Gurdjieff's allegorical idiom. But again I was criticized:

'You can't present such formulations to the general public. They are valuable for fifth-year Gurdjieff pupils.'

'I disagree. We heard these things in our first year. We aren't unique, there are other people like us who will respond as we did.'

'No public will take it, people will think you have lost your mind—so far are you from their world. "Oh, another cult!" they'll say. It's harmful to Gurdjieff to present him like this to a hostile, ignorant public.'

'I disagree again. I'm convinced that if everyone could begin with our beginning there would be less mystery-mongering, and less antagonism, from a hostile and ignorant public.'

'Gurdjieff's more elusive method was a necessary weeding-out. Some people must be eliminated at once, as those who have no place in them for these ideas.'

'True. But I'm writing for those who have. I believe the introduction we had is the ideal one.'

'Ideal for the mind alone. Not for incorporation of the knowledge.'

'That's another matter—the most important—and comes later. I leave incorporation and its mysteries for the next chapters. For the moment, remember this: "Some people have a nose for these ideas. In others there is nothing that Gurdjieff can touch. But there are a few people in each generation who are alive". . . .

'And another thing. I have seen dozens of people turn away because of inept presentations of Gurdjieff, but among those who were introduced to him as we were I have never seen *one* turn away.'

Whether I am right or wrong, here are a few of the summaries I made of the thinking that most influenced me. They give at least what Gurdjieff called 'a taste'. They can't be understood at once, but they contain a potent evocation—you can contemplate them as you do a painting which you like at first glance and of which you say, 'I'm not sure that I understand it, but I *feel* that I do.'

There is another factor. I must justify giving them at all.

Justification is necessary? Yes, I think so.

There has always been a general exhortation of silence—'Don't talk about Gurdjieff', 'Don't proselytize', 'Don't cast pearls', 'Don't reveal knowledge that will never be understood', etc., etc.

This admonition, I believe, has been responsible for most of the misunderstanding that exists about Gurdjieff—the hush-hush attitude, the mystification, the scepticism concerning his mission and his stature.

Several derogatory books have been published about him, and I've seen no refutation of them. Ouspensky, Nicoll and others have written books in his intention, and they have been notable. Thus a precedent has been established against the silence. But books that report a great deal about the daily work of Gurdjieff groups seem to me to leave a great void—that of an abstract introduction which would have illuminated the given concrete details.

Can I imagine anyone so pretentious as to claim a total understanding of Gurdjieff's knowledge? No, I can't. Or anyone so treacherous as to betray that part of it which can be revealed only by 'word of mouth'? No, again, I can't. But I can easily imagine someone so incensed over the slandering of Gurdjieff that he would attempt a corrective: not by trying to convey the teaching technique, but by indicating some of the ideas that lead *towards* the teaching.

This is my aim—an introduction, not an exposé. The best 'introducers' I knew were Orage and Jane Heap, and most of the abstractions I present here were made by Jane. She will never publish them, and I believe they should be heard if one is to talk about Gurdjieff at all. They are the ones I've found more illuminating to more people than any other presentation, and to me they are a requisite for an approach to a mind like Mauriac's.

I offer them in full consciousness that, even after their assimilation, you will have heard only a beginning of what must finally be understood, and of what must finally be achieved after it has been understood. Such formulations speak to the mind alone, and since the mind alone doesn't lead to the necessary 'changed course of life', it will be visible to anyone (I hope) how little I have violated the

prohibition of silence, and how much (I hope) I
may have helped to undo some of the harm that
has been unconsciously done.


## THREE CENTRES

We are flatteringly called three-centred beings, but
we have no future because we have two centres
filled only with our past habits.

Our centres are empty because we haven't filled
them consciously. Everything we have is passive.
The effort of this method is to make the three
centres work together.

Any activity for a human being that is less than
three-dimensional is sub-human.
We spend our lives wandering—escaping from one
error into another.

Life becomes always a discussion between three
centres: like or dislike, yes or no. All our time and
energy is wasted by this discussion.

Man is three different persons, three different up-
bringings, three different contents. We grow up
lop-sided—with each centre out-balancing the
others.

Only a small part of our life is under control. As we

are, we have no will. Will is a state of development —a possibility in a higher centre.

All we call development now is but an extension of one of the three centres. All our art is but an extension of the emotional centre, etc.

By *wishing* you can't add anything to your three centres—'By wishing a man cannot add a cubit to his stature.' You must have a method, a technique. Christianity was put into the Bible, but no technique for development was given. The technique is never written down.

Christ's public teaching was given in parable, leaving out the theory and the technique.

(In Gurdjieff's private teaching he presented both theory and technique.)

Every science has to draw upon a special vocabulary. The Gurdjieff vocabulary is as precise as that of any other science. All the terms in the Bible were once precise scientific terms: 'In my Father's house are many mansions', 'Turn the other cheek', 'An eye for an eye', 'The cross'. . . .

*This method:* a mathematical and material explanation of the creation, maintenance and purpose of the universe, man's place in that universe, his function and duty.

## The Unknown Doctrine

*Man's obligation:* to operate with the laws which operate the universe. Because man has a unique place. The obligation goes with that.

The awareness of your place is not a gift of nature. You must find it by conscious effort, not by hope. Man has a potentiality he knows nothing about. The science of ancient times. We have lost all idea of these potentialities.

Life provides no outlet for certain potentialities (Paul: the 'wall of partition'). Some people have forcible proof that they have potentialities for development.

Make an effort to develop a major organ: mental and emotional development.

Nature wanted to produce a self-evolving form. Man is the highest possible development of a self-evolving form. Nature can do no more; *we* must do it. All further development requires conscious effort. This requires labour comparable to that which nature has expended on our development so far, millenniums of it.

In all nature's creations, a certain activity follows a certain form.

We are an animal with a formless psyche. A psyche to have form must be three-fold.

There has been all knowledge in the world, but vast bodies of it have been wiped out (wars, calamities, etc.) as chalk off a slate. But all over the world we find proofs (if we can read) of a superior knowledge: Atlantis, Stonehenge, Pyramids, Mayan architecture, temples, etc.

Great cathedrals were built with a CONSCIOUS PURPOSE—to elevate for a moment the vibrations of people. This was a conscious attempt to leaven the masses.

*The Gurdjieff method:* A method of Conscious Effort and Voluntary Suffering against INERTIA and REPETITION.

## DEVELOPMENT AND GROWTH
### (THE DIFFERENCE)

A person is small, then he grows up.

Development is stages. A development takes place in our body: teeth. They're there, lying in the gums.

We've only become more educated; we haven't developed.

The beaver building its dam: physical-centre extension, not development.

Metamorphosis of caterpillar into butterfly: development, possibility of a soul.

Why does one follow this Method, the Fourth Way? If you feel dissatisfaction you'll try something—if you have a *need*. A need is an internal disequilibrium. You can tell by all your interests what your disequilibrium is. Because your interests are set going by your needs.

If we desire to develop, we do something about our two undeveloped centres. But if we don't find a method we run down scale. All our acts are appeasement because we haven't developed.

You've investigated methods, but you haven't *worked* in any method.

We all start equal before this unique activity.

You are sitting in a chair, comfortably. If you leave that chair without meaning to do this method's work, it is better not to leave it—you'll be standing all your life. Because you never get back to that first chair once you leave it—since life doesn't stand still.

## ASLEEP

Man is asleep.

In every religion, in all great literature, you find

references to the dream state. Must wake up (asleep in Adam, awake in Christ). All religions talk about being born again. We're asleep in the animal: the body is awake, the 'I' not.

This sleep is comparable to a hypnotic state. A child is put under the power of suggestion. Later in life, auto-suggestion. Complete mechanical state. Adults absolutely under a hypnotic spell—like fakir hypnotizing the rabbit; he controls the circulation of the blood. A river has a flow that's not so fast as the current. The hypnotist suggests to you a little faster than life suggests to you.

It's almost a desire of man to be asleep. We're so asleep that unless life becomes too difficult we don't wake up. A shock can waken you.

But you must find your reasons for wanting to wake up.

Study human mechanicality. When you see how mechanical you are you begin to awake—just as at the moment of waking from a dream you know you've been asleep.

Begin to compare your sleep and your waking state. After a dream you're embarrassed at exposure. In life you're exposed in the same way. You're willing to tell what a sorry figure you cut in a dream, but in life you excuse and gloss over.

No one can say how he's going to act under certain conditions. 'I know just how I'll act in that situation'—this is as wild as to say how you'll act in a dream.

In dreams you're running-down energy you didn't use up in the day.

If you've finished your day—if your centres have finished—you don't dream.

Study your dreams. There is a self-contained energy left over in one of the centres. You can discover in which centre you contain unused (during the day) energy: do you have predominately physical, emotional or mental dreams?

Emotional dreams wear us out most.

The three centres fall asleep separately. Sometimes at the beginning of sleep you jump violently. This is one centre letting go of another.

Our subconscious brain should be our conscious brain. Everything that has happened to us in life is there, penned up in the cerebellum, escaping only in sleep, trances, etc.

The conscious brain is polluted. Make an effort to tap the subconscious.

'The artist sometimes does this.'

'No, only fortune-tellers—sometimes; and unconsciously. To touch it unconsciously is dangerous.'

A CONSCIOUS effort to tap CONSCIENCE in the back brain.

## SELF-OBSERVATION

All great schools, all great systems of thought, all great religions have always striven to give man two freedoms: *inside* freedom (from vanity, self-love, etc.), and *outside* freedom (from 'education', etc.).

The first steps towards freedom are self-observation, to 'know thyself'. Gurdjieff's system begins with neutral scientific observation of one's self— taking notes on the body in the scientific manner. First the physical; later, notes on the mental and emotional centres.

The centre of gravity of *change*: you can't change by the mind alone; you must begin with the body, bring body and emotions into line.

The body is the only tool you have to work with. Make it a good tool. Resent the body's control of you.

Try to establish the physical as something apart

from the 'I'. The beginning of adult life is the knowledge that we have an 'I'.

Our bodies are fertilizers for a soul.

The personal equation between you and your body is pernicious.

If you woke up in the body of a unicorn you wouldn't know how to act. You are just as much at the mercy of your own body. You're not responsible for your behaviour—you're born embedded in an animal. (Yeats's poem: 'I am buried in a dying animal'.)

You think you know your body, but you don't even know when you scratch your head.

Our body is as much an object of the outside world as a tree, a plant, or a stone.

Say 'I *am*; I *have* a body'. The French have a better expression—they say 'I have cold', not 'I am cold'. We should be *conscious* of our bodies, *aware* of our emotions, *mindful* of our thoughts. Say 'I am having a passive thought', or 'I am having an active thought'.

Guard against self-deception, subjectivity, introspection. Introspection is bad—we have nothing to look into.

You've found how difficult it is to manage your body. Our minds don't move; our environment has paralysed our minds. Try exercises of mental stretching.

'We live bound in by our gestures. See how limited you are when you do the exercises. None of us has individual or essential gestures.'

'Won't doing a lot of self-observation make you self-conscious? Unnatural?'

'*Are* you natural? Break the mask. You can find out what is authentic. You'll enlarge your gestures, you'll enlarge your emotion, you'll eventually be able to control your environment.'

Our environment plays upon us. When Gurdjieff says 'Don't do as others do', he means: don't simply let your environment act upon you: think up something active to do.

## CONSCIOUS SUFFERING

Self-observation is conscious suffering.

We live only seventy years because of the useless suffering we submit to.

We must sacrifice automatic suffering.

Dig out your essence. Discover your type. This

will be an active alternative against unconscious behaviour.

Behaviourist phenomena is instinctive speech. It can be read by everyone around you.

HEREDITY has nothing to do with development. Heredity is simply: inclinations. Don't worry about it, just go on observing yourself.

Cast yourself for the rôle of a conscious human being. Act this rôle in public and private. *Recondition* yourself. Make every act purposive. Give play only to those ideas and emotions which are unassociated with 'personality'. This will counteract repetition.

Unconscious effort defeats us.

Most exercises only deplete your energy. Gymnastics that are not made to store energy (sport) wear out the physical centre. Boxers no good after thirty. Artists—who use emotion unintelligently—become pathological: have wasted their emotional centres. One-half the maladies treated by doctors only mean that *the centres* have been badly spent. Self-observation is the hardest of all things to do. It's the effort that counts—the remembering to do it.

'But *how* do you do it—by self-control?'

'No, not self-control—that uses up energy. Self-observation stores energy.'

'Do you do it by using suggestion?'

'No, suggestion won't help at all. Suggestion is simply keeping an idea in your mind. It is a passive thing. You must do an active thing.'

'Give an example.'

'Live a life of friction. Let yourself be disturbed as much as possible, but observe.'

'We're not accustomed to make such effort. We don't like friction.'

'Then no emotions are aroused. When there is no friction there is no development.'

'When you're upset can you observe better?'

'Yes. You're in a high state and can do it better.'

'But we self-observe all the time. It never stops.'

'On the contrary it never happens. It's the greatest effort man has ever undertaken. It's not congruous with the rest of our activities.'

'Actors self-observe.'

'An actor is the very worst observer. An actor may be *aware* of what he is doing, but there is a difference between self-awareness and self-observation. Self-observation is a self-directed activity; awareness is simply of the outside.

'To SEE is passive. To LOOK is active.'


## CHEMISTRIES

The Gurdjieff method: to release you from your inertias, to turn you against your obvious chemistries.

When you begin to do self-observation you have to admit you're helpless, you have to admit that everything governs you. The reason: because you are either attracted or repelled by everything, not only animate but inanimate.

Your whole life is a blind reaction to attraction and repulsion. Your world outlook can be changed by the slightest suggestion.

You are at a disadvantage with a person who repulses or attracts you.

Why are we always victims of certain people's chemistry? Everyone is, unless he's a catalytic. We are bundles of chemistry, of which we know perhaps ten chemical elements instead of 1,500.

With conscious effort a new chemical substance is made in one's organism that makes for understanding. You must make personal effort with a newly received idea—you create substances that way, a deposit of new chemical substances. Ideas are like food—must be eaten, digested, even cause nausea. To be sympathetic to ideas is nothing; sympathy is merely chemistry, not understanding. Sympathy = law of fusion of similarities; nothing new is deposited.

CONSCIOUS suffering is arrived at by putting

yourself in a situation agreeable to one centre and very disagreeable to the two others. Object: to get stretch, to get out of mechanicality, to find out what happens to your chemistry.

The exercise of self-observation produces a deposit in higher centres—higher mental, higher emotional, higher physical. It helps you to accumulate a force, a power—not a force that slides off you like water, but emanations that crystallize in you. You can do many things with this force.

What do you think you've done up to now? What have you rescued from this machine of repetition? What have you become purposive about, instead of being pushed into it by your chemicals, type, etc.?

Self-observation: you store energy for another purpose: *quality* rather than *quantity* vibrations.

### 'CHIEF FEATURE'

One of the great chief features is always self-love —complete self-love.

Scales. The little thing you put on the scales that tip them down is usually your chief feature.
Your chief feature is an outgrowth of your emotional attitude towards yourself.

Chief feature is never a good thing, but, once found, it can be used consciously.

*Our questionnaires:* to discover the motivating force back of all your acts.

Don't try to get rid of your motivating force when you find it, but use it to study yourself.

An investigation of pretences. Are you proud of your greatest weakness? Are you always stating your outstanding weakness in terms of strength?

The best way to begin to 'remember' what we are is sincerely to stop inventing those things we are not. We invent to hide ourselves.

Under very strong emotion sometimes we really do see ourselves.

Your development depends on your willingness (and speed) in acknowledging what's in you.

Vanity= a foolish display of what you haven't got.

Pride is more legitimate; it is in relation to what you've earned.
Vanity belongs to the body.
Self-pride is psychical pride.
Don't mix them.
No method can help you until you can get rid of vanity and self-pride.

There's something in you that is never fooled—you have an exact valuation of what you are.

Most of our troubles are caused by the inability to realize emotionally what we understand intellectually. That causes in us a clash of tempos—one centre is raised to high intensity, the two others out of harmony with it. This depends on your chief feature.

## ESSENCE AND MASK

We are 1 per cent ourselves, 99 per cent sociological.

There is the essence (the 'I'), and the representation (the personality).

The personality is the mask you've made to hide your essence.

*The mask.* Very difficult of discovery. Everyone has reasons for protecting himself.

You don't have to lose your mask if you don't want to. But *know* it. You can alter it when you know it. You can't alter anything without knowing it.

It's practically impossible for anyone to arrive at his essence. But by slow and patient work essence can be developed. It's developed by conscious effort.

Essence is the material of which the universe is made. Essence is divine—the particle of God in our subconscious is called Conscience.

Understanding is according to essence, not according to personality.

A person gives off radiations and emanations. The essence of a person is an emanation. Man has octave upon octave of emanations.

## EMOTION

An examination of the emotional centre, in view of producing a higher emotional body:

Emotion is a force, a chemical agent, a heat. We have only wishes, impulses, and appetites.

Emotions are the most valuable things we have, but they can be very cheap in expression.

What kind of emotion are you trying to express? Try to know what you're feeling.

Is the emotion justifiable? Inappropriateness of emotion is embarrassing. Often when people think they're intense it is painful for the onlooker—like the arrow that is spent instead of going to the target.

Then there is the degree of expression—the articulateness of it. Has the person finesse in expressing his emotion? elasticity?

64

Intensity is of value and it should be obvious whether the emoting creature has it or not—or whether he is just making a noise, giving his solar plexus gymnastics. Professional tears.

The human race is in decline because of useless emotion. Make a gratuitous experience one day—do something that's too hard to do: a conscious emotion.

Your physical body changes according to your emotions. It is the real barometer of your emotions. Temperament usually means lack of decision. Vascillating emotions make temperament.

We're occupied with ephemeral emotions. They come to us—we don't bring them on. Think certain thoughts, do gratuitous acts—this brings on emotions consciously—emotional stretching. List how many emotions come to you automatically, mechanically.

Emotion today is merely fermentation. *Observe* and you may get an idea during the observation. This changes the centre of gravity: a 'conversion'.

*Self-feeding:* to seek out emotions, thoughts, that are apropos to a mind.

The universe feeds itself.
With us: everything eats everything else.

When we don't do self-observation we eat ourselves.

A cat has a fully developed emotional body. A cat is spirited. Also a horse. 'Spiritual' is bad use of the word 'spirited'.

The emotional body makes the *spiritedness* of a person. The spiritedness of a spirited horse is obvious in relation to the disguised and veiled spiritedness of a cat. The flaming nostril is the end of the horse's spiritedness, but a cat flies into a towering rage. Same thing with people. Don't confuse sprightly gestures with spiritedness.

One hasn't muscles, only flesh, if one hasn't stress.

In America and England the emotional centre is repressed. A furtive emotional life. Anglo-Saxons have no education in the emotional centre, no training.

The mental centre has a vocabulary: spirit.
The emotional centre has a tempo: heat.
The physical centre has a power: force.

The psychology of the future will focus upon the emotional centre. Very difficult to do anything about the mind until we know more about electricity.

## MIND

Intelligence is an arrangement in the nervous centres—not arrived at by life but given you at birth.

Mind is posterior and superior to speech. Mind is the faculty of taking thought. Its real process is pondering. The subject-matter should be large true facts: the organization of the universe, etc. Its object is to group these ponderings into great wholes. But we cannot hold before our minds for one second the whole evidence about anything.

Divine reason: everything seen at once. Simultaneity. Ideas with form.

Mind is an active faculty. Take your impressions actively.

Our mind is like an intricate mechanical arrangement—electricity. Calls and responses (stimuli)—without a master.

Our reason at present: simply a post-mortem on an irrational act. Real reason is developed by opposition to repetition and inertia.

We waste our lives in associations, chiefly associations of words. Think at night of your words. Our words are aped.

The greatest poets have no experience of nine-tenths of their words. Sometimes a simple peasant can say in ten words something that a poet says in a hundred words full of air. The poets have been our downfall.

Artists, religionists, scientists have tried to think in forms (not formulas, but form—like painting). An idea of three centres = a form.

The idea of *man as an idea* is a form.

Every situation in the world is like a problem in mathematics—has a positive, a negative, a neutral force (active, passive, neutralizing). The neutralizing force is the form-giving force.

## RELIGION

'All the great general religions (created, as history itself testifies, by men of equal attainment in regard to the perfecting of their Pure Reason), are always based on the same truths. The difference in those religions is only in the definite regulations they lay down for the observance of certain details and of what are called rituals; and this difference is the result of the deliberate adoption by the great Founders of those which suited the degree of mental perfection of the people of the given period.'

Gurdjieff has also written: 'It is not a question of to

whom a man prays, but it is a question of his faith Owing to faith alone there appears in a being the self-consciousness necessary for him and also the valuation of personal Being as a particle of everything existing in the universe. Faith is conscience, the foundation of which is laid in childhood. If a man changes his religion he loses his conscience, and since conscience is sustained by his faith and his faith by his religion, therefore I respect his religion and for me it would be a great sin if I should judge his religion or disillusion him in it and thereby destroy his conscience which can only be acquired in childhood.'

You must formulate your idea of GOOD and EVIL. If you are holding up a cosmic scheme you are evil.

*Objective Good and Evil:* Understanding and effort = Right.
Failure to achieve them = Evil.

*By Objective is meant:* permanent knowledge.
*By Subjective is meant:* someone sits down in his armchair and makes up a system.

Obedience to any sociological system, to any religion, or to anything else not arrived at objectively = police regulations, traffic rules only.

The Bible: the self-regeneration of man.

We should spend our lives upgrading energies.

This is the hidden meaning behind alchemy. *To be born again.*

For rebirth there is an exact science, the greatest in the world, and its *technique* is sacredly concealed. ('Bind up the testimony, seal the law among My disciples'.) This prohibition was laid upon our race because information gives mind knowledge only, and mind knowledge tends to reduce the possibility of acquiring knowledge of one's being.

'Testament' means 'I will to you'. The Old Testament, the New Testament = knowledge willed to us.

What is this knowledge? It is the fulfilment of potential Being in every being: three-brained beings. This is the purpose of the universe.

The universe made flesh: Christ.

John the Baptist is the 'I' crying in the wilderness of the body.

Adam: the unregenerate man—living in the first *do* of the octave, living mechanically.

Development cannot begin until degeneration is arrested.

This is a method to obliterate death. Our supreme effort is reproduction: a succession of bodies in ourselves—a psychological objective continuance of individuality.

*Two kinds of immortality*—the two births: (1) automatic and (2) conscious.
Horizontal line: physical reproduction: heirs.
Vertical line: succession of one's self; the self-generation of man.

Immortality is a potential fact. The potential is always more full of possibilities than the actual.

We prepare our future by the way we use our energy. Every 24 hours we're given a supply of energy. If we don't do something about it today, we can't in a year.

'*Sins of the fathers*': you did something yesterday, you pay for it ten years hence. You are your own *fathers* in this.

When we die the vibrations that hold us together go into space. The vibrations of the physical organs run down the scale and go into the earth.

But the 'I' comes and comes until it develops.

If you develop yourself, Gurdjieff says, you become an individual instead of one of the thousand leaves on a tree. You become a seed.

*The Gurdjieff theory:*

## The Unkown Doctrine

All things in life work on two laws—3 and 7.
All psychological things fall within the law of 3
(the trinity).

All material things fall within the law of 7 (the
octave).

# V

# A LIFE FOR A LIFE

Y AIM in writing *The Fiery Fountains*—the
part called 'A Life for a Life'—was to
show how one proceeds, by stages and
degrees, to incorporate the knowledge we had been
given in abstract form.

Remembering certain words of Orage's, my
conception of the book was that it should employ
other means than dialectic. Somewhere he had
written:

Persuasion by dialectic is not only resistible, but what
is done by its means can be undone by the same means.
Persuasion, in short, is precarious. The 'sublime', on the
other hand, does not persuade; it overpowers, seizes and
holds captive; it is irresistible, and its effects are permanent; for what is admired has more lasting influence
than what is only reasonable.

Thus the idea of finding an art form in which to
tell my story would, I thought, guarantee its being

'admired' and give it an influence beyond the merely rational.

I began it with the simple history of our *Little Review* days and aspirations, and with great effort managed to cast the whole experience into a form that I felt touched the art of evocation. I shall never forget how difficult it all was, but I had three months in which to work and I worked with an intensity that seemed to spring from some inner resource that felt like inspiration.

In the early days of the *Little Review* people used to tell me that I had no critical sense, that I didn't know one thing from another. I always answered: I know the difference between life and death—in everything. This is all I wanted to know, this gave me my superabundance of superiority. We, the superiors, made experience out of nothing, we made life out of ourselves. We never found so much excitement outside as inside, we didn't travel because strange lands weren't as fascinating to us as ourselves. We could buy photographs of the Taj Mahal, but we couldn't recapture the conversations we might fail to have if we spent our time hurrying off to see such monuments. We were the people who knew things without learning them; we were the producers, rather than the product, of experience; our environment didn't condition us, we moulded our environment; enthusiasm was our validity, we knew nothing about throwing cold water—except on the mediocre; bourgeois-ism went down before us as in a strong wind; we threw out the uninteresting and raised the interesting to incandescence; we didn't pass through thought to arrive at opinion, we leapt to resplendent conclusions; words were too slow for us, we travelled by e-motion. To me our superiority was so undisputed that I was over forty before I found anything that could challenge it.

My most intense days in this personal calendar were lived in California. Jane Heap had joined the *Little Review* and we were publishing it from a ranch house near Muir Woods, across the bay from San Francisco. We brought out a number made up of sixty-four blank pages, announcing that we had found no art to publish, that we hoped to find some for the next number.

We had never thought of art simply as painting, poetry, music, sculpture. We thought art was an expression, through the arts, of a need of something else. It was about this something else that we talked all those summer days. I remember the eucalyptus trees in the sun, the path beside them where we began to talk in the morning, walking up and down from the house to the barn. We walked up and down all day. When the sun set I used to feel that the day had been perceived by us alone on earth, for surely no other people had spent all of it, as we had, in wondering about the world.

From California we moved with the *Little Review* to New York. In summer we had a small grey house in Brookhaven, Long Island, where questions and answers went on for ever. Under the blue locust trees, in shadows of sun and mist, we continued our shadowy speculations.

During this time we had read a book by Claude Bragdon which announced a coming book by a man named Ouspensky. It appeared, under the title of *Tertium Organum*, and we considered that we had found a contemporary author with a great mind. But what interested us most about Ouspensky was the rumour that he was associated with a greater man called Gurdjieff. Ouspensky was supposed to be writing a book about this man and his ideas which would be called *The Unknown Doctrine*.

Alfred Richard Orage, former editor of the *New Age* in London, came to New York as the precursor of this doctrine. He had just spent two years in France studying with the great man—so the story went—and if New York showed any interest in the doctrine the legendary Gurdjieff himself might come.

We went to the small theatre where Orage was to talk, with a feeling that our lives had waited always for what might be said there. Everyone we knew was in the audience—artists, intellectuals, socialites. We sat rather far back, I remember, because we wanted to watch the reactions of the audience. Mrs. Philip Lydig and Dr. Percy Stickney Grant sat just in front of us, Claude Bragdon across the aisle.

Orage walked out upon the stage. He was tall and easy, but quick and sure—the most persuasive man I have ever known. He sat down and began to tell, simply, why he had come. Claude Bragdon interrupted by standing up to say that he had a letter from Ouspensky which he would like to read. It was a conventional letter, everyone was bored, Bragdon was unaware of boredom as he began commenting on the letter. Orage stopped him expertly and went on with his talk. But the ease and flow of the evening had been broken. 'Talk louder,' someone called out. 'And be more interesting,' Mrs. Lydig said loudly. This made me angry. 'Don't do that,' I whispered to her—'What's the matter?' she said, still loudly, 'don't you agree?'—'Of course not,' I said, 'just wait, he'll be so interesting he'll be incomprehensible.' But he wasn't. He had no intention of being merely 'interesting'.

We went with Orage afterwards, to a Child's restaurant, and asked him all the questions we had been hoarding. By midnight we had learned that this doctrine would not fulfil our hopes, it would exceed them.

And then Gurdjieff himself came.

It was announced that the Gurdjieff group would give its special 'dances' in the Neighbourhood Playhouse, and all New York gathered again. Orage read explanatory notes for each dance, and everyone in the audience (except the genus intellectual) realized that he was in the presence of a manifestation which had its roots in a source of which we know nothing. Our sense of this phenomenon was so sharp that we almost forgot about the man Gurdjieff, who was supposed to be somewhere behind the scenes directing the dances. From my seat down front I saw him for a moment in the wings, commanding his pupils, exhorting them to greater, and ever greater, precision. When we went back later to find Orage I had just time to look carefully at a dark man with an oriental face, whose life seemed to reside in his eyes. He had a presence impossible to describe because I had never encountered another with which to compare it. In other words, as one would immediately recognize Einstein as a 'great man', we immediately recognized Gurdjieff as the kind of man we had never seen—a seer, a prophet, a messiah? We had been prepared from the first to regard him as a man different from other men, in the sense that he possessed what was called 'higher knowledge', or 'permanent knowledge'. He was known as a great teacher and the knowledge he had to offer was that which, in occult books and in the schools of the East, is given through allegory, dialogue, parable, oracle, scripture, or direct esoteric teaching. From what Orage had told us we knew that Gurdjieff presented his knowledge in a terminology which would not alienate the factual minds of Western thinkers. We had never been ranged among the factual; but neither had we ever been, nor could we ever be, satisfied with the purely mystical or metaphysical.

We looked upon this man standing in the wings of the Neighbourhood Playhouse in New York City as a messenger between two worlds, a man who could clarify for us a world we had hoped to fathom—the world which the natural scientists had revealed but not interpreted.

I think I really thought of Gurdjieff, at first, as a sort of Hermes, teaching his son Tat. But while it was impossible to understand the Hermetic dialogue, merely by reading it or speculating about it, I felt that the essence

A Life for a Life

of the Emerald Tablet itself might be made understandable to us through Gurdjieff's method of teaching. What
I mean exactly is this: that what philosophers have
taught as 'wisdom', what scholars have taught in texts
and tracts, what mystics have taught through ecstatic
revelation, Gurdjieff would teach as a science—an exact
science of man and human behaviour—a supreme science
of God, world, man—based on sources outside the scope,
reach, knowledge or conception of modern scientists and
psychologists.

Later, at Carnegie Hall, another series of dances was
given. Plans had been made for an accompaniment of
four pianos but as it turned out there was only one,
played by M. de Hartmann with the percussive splendour demanded by Gurdjieff. These dances were taken
from, or based upon, sacred temple dances which Gurdjieff had seen in the monasteries of Tibet, and their
mathematics were said to contain exact esoteric knowledge. New York was still interested, but the intellectuals
had begun to complain that the performers' faces didn't
register 'joy' as they danced. I suppose these critics would
have been pleased by an Isadora Duncan expressiveness
over the movements of the planets in space.

We spent all the time we could with Orage, listening
to the ideas of Gurdjieff. And then one night Gurdjieff
himself talked. He presented his ideas as not new but as
facts always known and always hidden—that is, never
written down but passed from age to age through the
teachings of the great initiates. 'Initiate' had always been

a word that left us cold, if not hotly antagonized, because of the nebulous thinking of the people who used it. But now we had no time to waste in revolt over words. The substance of Gurdjieff's doctrine was, for all of us, for the first time, an answer to questions.

All our lives our questions had been, we thought, everyman's questions; but everyman seemed satisfied with answers which didn't satisfy us. If a great scientist said, 'We can erect a coherent system dealing with all aspects of human knowledge and behaviour by the refinement, extension and continued application of the methods which have been so successful in the exact sciences,' we said, 'No, you can't, there's something you won't be able to get at with those methods.' If a great doctor said, 'Prayer is power,' we said, 'Yes, it must be, but why?' If a great philosopher based his doctrine on the 'incalculable forces of the spirit', we knew what he was talking about, but the phrase was vague. What *are* those forces? What more, if anything, can be learned about them? We found more meat in Hermes: 'For the Lord appeareth through the whole world. Thou mayest see the intelligence, and take it in thy hands, and contemplate the image of God. But if that which is in thee be not known or apparent to thee, how shall He in thee be seen, and appear unto thee by the eyes? But if thou wilt see Him, consider and understand the sun, consider the course of the moon, consider the order of the stars.'

But since astronomers had no revelations to make (except physical ones), and since no philosopher had ever spoken clearly about what it is to 'know thyself', we were left stranded. All we could do was to reiterate: in that region between physics and philosophy is there no firm ground for the mind's construction of a faith?

Gurdjieff's statement was that there does exist a super-knowledge, a super-science; and what he had to say about it convinced us that we would never hear anything else to compare with it, never find anything else which could illuminate the great texts to which we had always wanted to give a reverent investigation.

When he spoke of the 'way' in which this knowledge could be acquired—a way which brought you gradually into a 'condition of knowledge'—we were ready to believe that it might indeed be a way for us. But though we suspected the magnitude of the knowledge, we didn't realize how different its development and application would appear to us fifteen years after our first encounter with it. And we certainly hadn't the faintest idea how difficult this particular 'way' would sometimes be.

After his appearance in New York Gurdjieff left for France where, in Fontainebleau-Avon, he had established his 'Institute for the Harmonious Development of Man'. People from all parts of the world, to whom his cosmology had become a way of life, were living and working in the Institute. Orage and the group that had come to New York were returning with Gurdjieff.

And so it was that in June 1924, Georgette, Jane, Monique and I—as well as several other people who felt as we did—left New York for Paris. We knew the import of our decision: we had prepared to 'cast aside our nets' and follow.

*Fontainebleau-Avon*. From the station we walked down the road to Avon, to the end of the village where a forest begins. At the right was a garden door in a high wall. Jane pulled the bell and it tinkled long and softly. A boy with alert eyes opened the door, smiled without curiosity, and asked us to come in. He said that Mr. Gurdjieff had driven to Paris, would be back for dinner; would we walk through the gardens where we would find our American friends.

We entered a grass courtyard enclosed by the *château* and the wall. It had the aspect most becoming to courtyards—that of a garden half-abandoned. In the centre was a fountain; its gentle water dropped upon stone night and day. The boy led us through the *château*, which had once belonged to Mme de Maintenon and was now called the Château du Prieuré. It was not wide but long, its *salons* opened both upon the entrance court and the formal gardens in front. Beyond were forests which led over pine-lined roads to the village of Moret, on a lovely river with the unlovely name of Loing.

We stood for a long time on the terrace, among urns and balustrades and all the brighter flowers, drinking in once more the divine light and air of France. The gardens were long, a fountain sprayed their stillness, and beyond them were stone benches under an arbour of yew trees (perhaps not yew, but I always felt they were). The kitchen gardens were far in the distance and we found our friends there among the vegetables.

They took us through the *château* and indicated vacant rooms we were to choose from. The principal bedrooms were over the *salons* and some American had named this wing the Ritz. It was used for transient guests. Two other floors, with small bedrooms, were called the Monastery. We chose our cells here, mine over the dining-room garden, Georgette's towards the forest. Jane chose a room at the back that looked into a farmyard, because she liked to be wakened by crowing cocks. Here there was a small stable that had already become a legend because Katherine Mansfield, during her last illness, had lain in the loft, breathing the healthy smell of cows and hay.

At dinner there were perhaps twenty people at the table; others, responsible for the feast, ate nearer the kitchens. We were surprised to see Ouspensky among the guests, having heard that he had left the Institute for good. On this first night we were curious about Ouspensky. He sat at Gurdjieff's left and acted like a small boy, laughing more than he meant to, saying what he meant not to, flushing with the armagnac forced upon him. This situation wasn't to Ouspensky's detriment, it is the lot of everyone who passes through the Gurdjieff life-class. As we learned later, the ritual of toasts, in armagnac, had to do with the psychology of human types. And since important matters were never explained to you in this school until you yourself came upon them—through long experience and repetition *ad nauseam*—it took me many years to understand the hierarchy of the toasts, or

to apply it to myself and others with even the beginning
of accuracy. Though Ouspensky must have taken part
in this ceremony a hundred times, I always felt that he
had never discovered its significance; that he knew ideas
but didn't know people. Gurdjieff's doctrine of the 'unknown' began with man the unknown.

The doctrine was embodied in an enormous manuscript on which Gurdjieff was working day and night.

During our first months at the Prieuré, Gurdjieff was
personally inaccessible—at least to our group. We saw
him at mealtime, in the study-house after dinner during
the dances, in the *salon* for readings of the manuscript, at
café tables in Fontainebleau for the translation of new
chapters, sometimes in his car for trips which most
people hoped to avoid, as they were nerve-racking. But
he wasn't available for personal communication or instruction. He had finished one phase of teaching and had
not yet begun upon the next.

Even now I cannot attempt to describe Gurdjieff. I
would feel as if I had been asked to write a description
of Nature in all her moods. And I cannot talk of the
material of his teaching, of its method or its meaning. I
can tell what it did to me, that is all. It is adjusted
differently to every individual, and everyone would tell
of it differently. It is completely different from what I
imagined it would be, from what I understood it to be,
stage by stage. It is a story of a new education, of taking
whatever degree your heredity and upbringing, your
wish and your will, make possible. It has no relation to
psycho-analysis or any of the other modern intro-

spections. Introspections into what? into what non-existence? It is a cleansing and a filling. Its science consists in the precision with which you are charted, by which you are aided—slowly enough not to break you, fast enough to keep you in that state of wonder, surprise, shock, torment, remorse, reward, which alone taps your potential forces. The first statement I heard Gurdjieff make about his teaching was: 'I cannot develop you; I can create conditions in which you can develop yourself.'

The Institute had been in operation for two or three years before we arrived and I remember the people who were working there as some of the most interesting people I have ever known. One especially, from Constantinople, became a great friend of ours. In her outer manifestations she personified what they had all tried to attain—a holding-in rather than a going-out. She was a genial kind of person but she always made you conscious of a silence in her. She didn't tell you what she 'thought' about anything. At first this puzzled and exasperated me; I still measured people by expressiveness and thought by expression. I decided that she didn't think, or that she was inarticulate. Later I noticed that she talked rather vaguely of anything at all until she was questioned. Then she answered with economy, holding herself to the frame of your question, offering no more than it called for. After a few weeks of this technique I came to feel a power in it. This woman didn't thrust herself at you, it was as if she realized that one has very little self to thrust. She gave you no stories of her inner life, she seemed to know that no one has any inner life worth mentioning. Of course there were other people in the group who had mastered few or none of the realities that were being taught. They were as vain as people everywhere in life who express their 'personalities' at all times.

Orage was at the Prieuré when we arrived. He and his wife, with several other pupils from New York who had been there before, formed our immediate group; but there were also new people from France, England, Germany and points east. According to type, each got something, nothing, or everything out of being there. Everyone who came knew the fantastic stories of the Institute's purpose which had been imagined and reported —from vague spiritual interpretations to the definitely gross ideas of certain Frenchmen or the naïve generalizations of certain Americans.

One of our New York friends, a *Little Review* contributor, stayed at the Prieuré only one day. She asked intellectual questions and received allegorical answers. She began to feel spiteful. 'If there's anything in all this,' she said, 'someone can put it into a phrase for me. Otherwise I won't know whether I'm for it or not.' None of the Gurdjieff people tried to put anything into a phrase, though Jane did her best by saying, 'It's a method to keep your past from becoming your future.' Our New York friend ignored this. 'I don't know why they won't talk,' she said, 'I asked the least anyone can ask.' No one disputed this and she left the next day. Fourteen years passed before I saw her again, when she came into Michaud's to dine one night and sat at our table for coffee. I didn't know what she thought about anything at this time, but when she thought of us she evidently thought of religion because she said, 'Still learning to be good?' I didn't know what to answer, I could think of no phrase that would catch her attention. Instead of speaking I sat and thought about her, and fourteen years, and observed the sadness of life. It wasn't that she looked older, her face was unlined and her vitality unworn. But fourteen years of the same reflexes, mannerisms, reactions, gestures, postures, expressions, had traced their paths on her psyche as associations plough through the grey of the brain. I knew in advance exactly what she would say, having heard it in the years before, so I didn't listen: instead I watched her mannerisms announce in advance what she would say. This pantomime, unconscious and sculptural, composed a tragedy. When a line formed at the corner of her mouth and drew it down in a bitterness deeper than ever before, I knew that she was going to say, 'Well, that's the way it is.' It was like watching an actor walk upon a stage in the role of Vanity, giving a photographic performance of the visible signs of self-love upon the organism. But what impressed me most was the length of time that passed between the beginning and the end of the mouth's gesture and the beginning of the spoken phrase. It hadn't been so long, years ago; now it seemed a full minute. I thought of someone's definition of Gurdjieff's teaching as a 'method of acceleration'. I thought of all the kinds of acceleration I had watched since my first contacts with people who had accelerated.

# A Life for a Life

Of all the people who came to the Prieuré while I was there, no one was ever asked to stay if he wanted to leave, and no one was asked to leave if he really wished to stay. Some were not received at all. One well-known woman came out from Paris expecting to be received as a celebrity. Gurdjieff didn't know who she was but he saw her from a window when she arrived. She was told he wasn't there. The story of his brief explanation of course went the rounds—at least to the three of us who always had our ears at the psychological keyhole: her vanity was too fixed, it would take years to break it up; she was not young, the chances were against success, his effort would be disproportionate since hers would probably be non-existent.

Another quick flight was made by an American woman who stayed only three days. She reacted to new situations as if they were old ones. This made her angry and she left in disdain. One of the most touching people who fled was the man who said he hadn't the courage to start on what might be only another wild-goose chase after knowledge. He left sadly. There was an English-woman who identified everything she heard with her own idea of Buddha, and then left to continue a life devoted to her own nebulous conception of 'know thyself'; and there was another woman who announced that you could find a hundred such teachers in the world, that this doctrine was no more interesting than any other. If we hadn't already heard enough to know its unique-ness (at least for our time and place in the world) we might have been influenced by all the cross-currents—

the people who called it and us too material, those who
said we were hypnotized, those who predicted our decline into mysticism or a sort of super-metaphysics. But
it would have taken a lot of effort to be influenced by
people who discovered only mysticism in the most lucid
formulations, and who sensed neither mystery nor
knowledge in the most paradoxical. So we simply got to
work on the doctrine, and on ourselves. And there was
nothing simple about either activity.

Outwardly, at the Prieuré, we felt that our days were
numbered. Inwardly we felt that we had been given a
key to a new model of the universe.

Outwardly we didn't go through any of the training
that the older pupils had demonstrated in New York.
That was over for the moment, Gurdjieff was finishing
the last chapters of his book, and everyone was absorbed
in translation from Russian into English, French, Ger-
man. Besides this we worked in the kitchen gardens, we
straightened garden paths. ('Too slow,' Gurdjieff said,
walking by, 'must find way to do in half time.') We cut
grass and helped to cut down trees. I had a small silent
portable piano which I sometimes took out under the
yew trees to practise on. 'Waste of time,' Gurdjieff said,
walking by with the musician, M. de Hartmann; 'must
find short cut.' I sought out the musician later, hoping
for interpretation. He began: 'Arensky had only four
fingers on one hand but he could play anything and play
it as he wanted to. Question of engineering.' Then he
gave me so much new information about techniques and

the mechanics of bodies in relation to instruments that I
was tempted to return to Art.

But I had not gone to Gurdjieff to learn more about
Art; I wanted to learn more about the universe. If anyone had asked me exactly what I wanted to find out, and
if I could have answered as simply as a child, I would
have said, 'I want to know what is God.' When I realize
now how I might have related this wish to an essential
conduct, and how I couldn't, I am appalled. If I had
known how to ask a question, if I could have been
simple (I who have always been so sure of simplicity), I
could have asked, 'What does it mean—"in My Father's
house there are many mansions"? What does it really
mean?' Or 'Will you tell me something about the Last
Supper?—why does religion seem to offer no real interpretation of this sacrament?' I wouldn't have received
answers that could be regarded as answers, since 'what'
and 'why' were always discouraged at the Prieuré and
only 'how' was sometimes rewarded; but I might have
started ten years earlier on that break-up of my own
image which precedes any *study* of man created in the
image of God. As it was, 'God' was not mentioned in
this place after the day when someone at the table suc-
ceeded in a direct question and Gurdjieff answered 'You
go too high.' I never found a way to overleap these
barriers, made for leaping. I had so much awe of all that
I heard, I was so convinced that I would learn what it
meant through some extension of the mind, that I could
think only of studying it, discussing it with everyone—
that is, continuing to live as I had always lived, by

imagining what I could of the ideas involved, hoping
that everyone else's imagination would work too, and
believing that if we thought and discussed long enough
we would come upon revelation.

I don't regret the endless discussions—these first years
of the Gurdjieff abstractions were a golden age to me.
But if you linger on in it you never arrive at essentials.
When you get beyond it you realize why all the stories
told about Gurdjieff's presentation of the Hermetic wisdom are surface stories. I have yet to see in print, even
in the two respectable articles written by men who have
worked with him, a single indication of the concrete
substance of his mentation. Someone writing anony-
mously said: 'For me the most sensational aspect of
Gurdjieff's work was a sort of sublime common sense. I
mean that my experience resembled many times those
of the initiate in antiquity who was asked by his friends
how he felt when he was told the secrets of an occult
brotherhood. "Like a fool", he said, "for not having
seen for myself the truths they taught." ' After my golden age I never felt this facility of seeing-for-one's-self.
'You don't mean that there's anything really secret about
this doctrine, do you?' people have asked me for years.
How answer such a question? In two ways perhaps.
Either there are no secrets, or—nothing but secrets.
Atoms aren't as secret as they were, someone has charted
them and broken them up.

But in 1925 I hadn't been bombarded and split up,
as the atom had. The Prieuré of my day was not the
Institute where pupils were wakened at all hours, pushed

beyond their second-wind into real fatigue, their life-habits turned into too-difficult new patterns. All this came to me later, in quite another form. The Prieuré I remember is a place where reverent study filled the days and nights. After dinner we went to the study-house— originally an aeroplane hangar from war days, later converted by Gurdjieff into a place for work. The floors were covered with oriental rugs and we sat on cushions arranged in two tiers around the walls. There was a large low stage on which pupils worked out the intricate sacred dances. Usually Gurdjieff began the evening at the piano, composing the music for a new dance-movement which M. de Hartmann scored simultaneously; then the pupils began to work it out under Gurdjieff's instructions, always given in a mental shorthand that sounded far too rapid to be understood. But the woman from Constantinople and several others translated the commands into movement almost as swiftly as M. de Hartmann had made the piano orchestration. Sometimes afterward, if there were guests who wanted to understand the aim of the Institute, Gurdjieff would talk. This talk was always geared to three audiences—the guests, the pupils, and Gurdjieff himself; that is, first, what the guests would make of it; what the pupils would learn of the guests and of themselves as they listened to Gurdjieff; and what Gurdjieff himself would learn of the guests and the pupils.

Afterwards we would go to our rooms and 'philosophize' over what we had heard. The subject-matter that so engrossed us was not material we had heard before, though we might have discovered it in Hermes, Buddha, the Bible, had we known how to. Gurdjieff's terminology was completely new; but what held our attention and stretched our minds was the body of knowledge to which the terminology was applied: study of man's psyche from the standpoint of an exact science, illuminating the mystery of the processes by which a man can be said to be born again.

'Unless a man be born again . . .'—this was the key-note of Gurdjieff's science, his work, his effort, his example. For this reason he had no patience with the man who merely 'philosophizes'; his interest was in the man who 'can do'. Later we were to understand a great deal about this distinction.

I see now that we lived those first great years of Gurd-jieff's teaching in clouds of conviction that we were *not* treating it as a philosophy. Because the ideas involved in this science were new to us, we thought our reactions to them were new. Because our minds were exploring this knowledge, we assumed that our hearts were under-standing it. We thought we had already outgrown those self-regarding inflations for which Gurdjieff had a one-word description: 'psychopathic'. We thought we were already well advanced on the road to self-knowledge. How far we still had to go even to make a start was, fortunately, hidden from all of us.

Life seems to be an experience in ascending and de-scending. You think you're beginning to live for a single aim—for self-development, or the discovery of cosmic truths—when all you're really doing is to move from place to place as if devoted primarily to real estate. Looking back I see myself *en voyage*, clutching my suitcase of Gurdjieff ideas, convinced that my only property lay inside it, but spending four-fifths of my time searching a home 'where we could really work'. In those brief intervals of home peace the real emphasis was on home rather than on cosmos. Of course we gave our minds to the latter and to the 'terror of the situation' presented by our inertias; but since inertia is man's tradition, could we by our own efforts 'push back civilization single-handed', as Orage so often said? We read and reread the Gurdjieff manuscript, but I began to feel that there must be something *to do* that we weren't doing. I still reacted to our meetings and discussions with exaltation, but I knew this state to be simply my capacity for being moved. Pushed to its extreme it becomes the mystic's ecstasy, anything can be believed in such a state. I was not made to be a mystic; I have always been sceptical of faith without science. The real object of this quest was surely that injunction about being born again. Were we approaching such a condition? I couldn't see that we were.

I didn't minimize the actual transvaluation of all values which seemed to me the most important by-product of our investigation—so important that I wanted to spend my time proselytizing for them. I thought people would take to great ideas as motors take to petrol. But they didn't, they simply continued to say, 'I'm all against this looking into one's self—it's dangerous.' 'Of course it may be dangerous,' I said, 'unless you keep on looking.'

I could never understand why they wouldn't face this danger as well as any other. Was it that what they saw in themselves frightened them more than other dangerous sights?

In trying to apply the Gurdjieff values to human behaviour, our most passionate arguments always took place over art and religion—since you can't convince an artist that art isn't mankind's noblest expression, and you can't convince a religionist that there exists a more elevated conception of Good and Evil than the one he holds. I have lost years of youth trying to persuade religionists that Boehme was right when he said, 'Anyone who hasn't learned that there is no more good (God) in one thing than in another is still a child.'

I remember one all-night struggle with a religious group which Jane summed up like this: 'You people are talking of an emotional experience—religion. You say we make a god of the mind because we are talking of something that is experience on three planes. Your emotional experience can be compared to a dog's joy in greeting his master. Because a dog has only two planes of experience. I'm not minimizing the dog's experience, but your statements reduce all humanity to animals.'

I continued to believe that all this talk would make people stop, look and listen. 'Why do you think so?' Jane said. 'Look at your results.' She was right, my results couldn't have been more disastrous if I had been advocating murder instead of self-development.

One day Orage asked me, 'Why are you always arguing about right and wrong?'

'Because I'm going to convince people,' I said.

'But you know you can't.'

'No, I don't. I believe that if I can present these ideas intelligently enough——'

'Good heavens,' he said, 'you don't really believe that people are ever convinced of anything by listening to ideas?'

'Of course I do,' I said. 'What other way is there?'

'There are only three ways of influencing people,' he said—'magnetization, competition, example.'

I was always running up against the injunction that 'by taking thought a man cannot add a cubit to his stature'. The Gurdjieff mentation was supposed to be the wedge that entered just here. 'The brain is not an organ with which to arrive at truth. The brain is just a muscle. "Mind" as we know it merely uses words, formulates reactions, runs out a chain of associations, repeats received ideas, stirs up a heap of impressions received passively.' This statement led to a summation: 'The first step in becoming an adult is to realize that things are done *to* us, not *by* us.'

There, within a sentence, was a concept with dimensions. There, within the framework of the concept, was the quintessence of a theory and a technique which Gurdjieff presented not as a unique theory but as a unique activity. There, in a single formulation, was expressed our adherence to this unknown doctrine in which, for the first time, we were hearing things that were not merely repetitions of things we had already heard.

I was quite willing, I thought, to give up my loyalty to the mind. But I wanted to be convinced, or to convince myself, that I was approaching a process higher than taking thought. I believed that if the potentiality of such a faculty existed we would find it in this doctrine. But I didn't for a moment believe we had yet done so. When would we? Why hadn't we already? Because of some obstacle, unknown to us, within ourselves? I hadn't yet the vision to know whether this was so or not; and, if it was, of what the obstacle consisted.

Of course I knew that this knowledge runs through all great legends, allegories, parables; that it can be found in the whole scale from fairy-tales to scripture; that it is suggested in all great systems of thought, in all great schools—Hermes, the Gnostics, the Essene monks, Pythagoras. . . . Of course, I kept saying to myself, we were digging out the findings and building up the parallels; we were learning why there is no real religion in the world, why the words of Jesus Christ have not been understood, why 'God is not known or worshipped, merely used'; why most religious interpretation has been distortion; why true religion means something else; why the something else is never written down, never referred to except under the protection of formal thought; why it is never offered for nothing, why a life must be given to find this Life. We thought we were ready to give our lives for it. But how were we to discover, unaided, the unwritten demand behind the immense abstractions? Of course we were being aided by Gurdjieff, but the aid was offered in those terms which I had not yet come to understand: 'I cannot develop you; I can create conditions in which you can develop yourselves.' What was it that we were to *do*, beyond trying to 'take impressions actively', so that things would be done by us, not to us? All the keys to this enigma were perhaps offered in the Gurdjieff manuscript but, as its author said, they were placed far from the locks.

I felt that all my speculation continued to be purely imaginative, and I knew that Orage had a definition of 'imagination' which left you without any pride in this faculty. 'Imagination as we use it,' he said, 'is simply an excess of desire over ability.'

In our desperate and impersonal self-examination we would meet for discussion and try to illuminate ourselves about ourselves. To all of us Jane's formulations for self-questioning were the most vital. She would present questions like the following and we would try to dig out the answers:

1. How much of your life is an illusion (the world as it appears to you through the distortions of lack of self-knowledge)?
2. How many failures or negative results (from well-intentioned, well-conceived, hopeful plans) do you think were caused by your illusion being too patent to others—with other illusions? Have you ever had a glimpse of the extent to which you rest under self-hypnosis? Have you ever been aware of the power of self-love as an hypnotic force?
3. Have you ever had a moment of realization of the spectacle of human beings going through life in a state of deep hypnosis?
4. Could you ever detach yourself enough from your illusory

world to conceive a world of Reality—in which each person
perceived Reality as one and the same thing—not interpreted
by the whims, vanities, likes and dislikes of a reacting animal?
but perceived by a permanent, understanding three-fold 'I'—
able to use the chemistry and vibrations of his type consciously
instead of always being acted upon from the outside (as we are)?

We asked Orage: 'Is contemplation the process higher
than taking-thought?'

'No,' he said. 'Contemplation is the last note in the
thinking octave, but only the first note in the octave of
a higher process.'

What interests me now, as I review our evolution in
the Gurdjieff teaching, is that for so long I never doubted
that all our talk and 'thinking' would provide the desired
self-development. Of course talk gives you almost as
much new gland life as being in love does. But why,
since I knew that being in love doesn't necessarily lead
to anything beyond being in love, did I assume that talk
inevitably leads to something beyond talk—for instance,
to Being? It took me so long to find the right answer to
this question that I have never since been able to look
back upon my thinking past with pleasure.

During most of these middle years of our great experience Gurdjieff was not easily accessible. It may be
that he would have been, if we had known how to need
what he had to offer.

In the autumn of one of these years we had to face a

fact that none of us knew how to face. Orage died. In England.

The year 1934 had come and we were still in Vernet when we heard that Gurdjieff was in Paris. Then came the news that he was accepting a small group for special teaching.

From Paris Solita sent me reports of this teaching—daily pages of her struggles through the almost unbearable tensions of trying to die to an old life. The effort to pass on this experience to me was a labour of love and I doubt that I, under the same circumstances, could have accomplished it for anyone, however much I might have wanted to.

As I reread these notes today I come upon a formulation in two words—a noun followed by a verb of such extensions that you feel you can never again regard any fact without examining it under the influence of this verb. Of course two words on a piece of paper are open to any interpretation that two thousand million people can give them. Everything, in the end, is interpretation. But *what* interpretation?

You can take three phrases like 'A tooth for a tooth, an eye for an eye, a life for a life' and interpret them in any way you like. But to knock out someone's tooth or pluck out someone's eye for your own lost tooth or eye, to kill someone because he has killed someone else—these retaliations can't be the meaning. No one ever gave me a hint, in my young days, that these three phrases present a picture, on three planes, of man's three inter-acting systems. We *do* have second teeth that replace baby teeth; we *do* develop an eye to see those things which are unseen; we *do* have to give up one kind of life to find another kind.

But no parents or teachers or religionists seem to know the under-meanings. They simply say, 'The words of Jesus are clear and cannot be misunderstood by anyone who wants to understand them.' Wants to—and then what?

Up to this point in my pilgrim's progress I had tried to build my thinking on the following model: 'Think large true facts, seen as forms—such as the organization of the universe. Forms of thought are energies. Think: from birth to death we are immersed in actions, we fitfully guide ourselves away from or towards things; we cannot hold before our minds for one second the whole evidence about anything. The mind's object is to grasp the facts as wholes. Elevate yourselves. Seek out emotions and thoughts that are appropriate to a mind. That is self-feeding. Everything eats everything else—the universe feeds itself.'

The statement that most fired my imagination, I remember, was this one: 'After a certain rate of vibration everything in the universe becomes psychological. Air and light=psychological food. The transmutation of substances.'

But what was I to do with this thought? I couldn't *think* beyond the fact that the visible physical world is the physical body of the universe. Then I must bring in

'As above so below.' All right, I too have a physical
body—I can see it.

All right, then the next step must obviously be: 'The
human body is given you to understand the universe.
All right. Next: 'We are made up of, are replicas of, the
universe.' Well, if the human body 'is made like an
electric station, generating and wasting energy', it is here
that that transmutation of substances comes in. Transmutation would lead to a very great thought: 'the self-
regeneration of man: an effort at reproduction—a succession of bodies in ourselves, each of a higher vibration.'
In other words, immortality? Well, all right. I certainly
know that I have something more than a physical body.
I have an emotional body and a mental body. But how,
in thought, am I going to relate these bodies, which I
can't see, to higher substances of the universe, which I
can't see? No, thought comes to an end. Try images,
then. All right: man made in the image of God. But I
couldn't complete the image. Beyond thought and image I was waiting, waiting for that knowledge-to-come
of As-Above-So-Below, which I felt would one day
burst upon me in a blinding light. In a way it seemed so
simple an image that no one could fail to construct it
step by step. In another way it seemed that no man
would ever do it, that we would continue to exist only
'in relation to a mystery'.

November, December, January, February, March
were still to come and Georgette and I were to spend
them in Vernet, out of contact with the man in Paris

The Author, 1929.

Jane Heap, New York, 1918, at the time of the *Ulysses* trial.

Georgette Leblanc, 1932.

Solita Solano, 1930.

Orage in the 1920s.

Mrs. Enrico Caruso, 1945.

Gurdjieff, taken in France in the year of his death, 1949.

who was helping a group of people step by step into the knowledge of that process higher than taking thought.

I was so tormented by our absence from this source that I began to dream of our predicament. I hadn't dreamed for years, but now I had a dream like an old mystery play. In it we were slaves, but at the same time we were actors in a drama, in which the roles had been distributed for conscious playing. We walked as a pageant through life, yet we were walking on a stage. There were two columns at its ends, with wide steps between them leading away from the audience. We came on at the left, in a long procession, walking slowly. At the centre of the stage we turned our backs to the audience and walked down the steps. When it came my turn I was too tired to go beyond the first step, I sat down on it to rest. The slaves behind me were held up, they tried to push me on, crying that I would be beaten if I stayed there. I said, 'We are such tortured people, we can bear no more.' Then I noticed that I was sitting with my hands on my knees, that I had raised my head and was looking straight out before me. In a flash there passed through me a vision, like those told by mystics, of ineffable impression, in which the meaning of all life appeared to my consciousness. I thought: I may never again see this as a whole, such total impression cannot happen often, it is like a picture of hope. I began to call out to the other slaves, 'There is hope, there is hope, we can work for Being.' They crowded around in fear and tried to quiet me. 'You must not speak of it aloud, they

A Life for a Life

will kill us.' I went on crying loudly until an old slave pushed through the crowd and took my hand and led me to the bottom of the steps. He asked the others to gather round and we all sat down in a circle about him. We were now sitting at the bottom of the steps, invisible to the audience. Then in a quiet voice, so that no one else would hear him, the old man began to address us. 'Is there anyone here', he said, 'who can say he knows what is meant by love of God?'

This dream only increased my trouble. It was precise in its symbolism, it pictured my stranded state. I began to compose self-indictments: 'Why don't I know what to do? The answer must be that I don't believe in these ideas enough, or that I am no longer capable of acting on my beliefs. Why don't I believe enough? I am convinced that nothing else makes sense. If I continue to ask "Does anything make sense?" I know that asking this question for years is no way of finding an answer to it. Then what in the name of sense holds me back? Why don't I begin to work? Why does the thought of it paralyse me? Why do I hold back longer than before a plunge into a cold lake?'

I could have answered that I really didn't know what to do, and could by no means find out. I knew of course that there was always a 'work' to do—that difficult work of trying to 'know yourself' by observing yourself. So in Vernet I decided to perform this exercise more conscientiously.

I remembered Orage saying, 'Make a list of all the

facts you know about yourself. Perhaps then you can begin on your unknowables.'

But I had made many analyses of my nature, and I asked myself what good they did. Gurdjieff had said that one's nature never changes; that is not the change you can affect. I knew that really to observe yourself scientifically, you were supposed to do another kind of examination. It consisted of not thinking, not feeling, but trying to *see* what happens; not constating what you thought or felt or imagined—all this being invisible to an on-looker; but trying to see yourself move and speak as you can see actors on a film-screen moving and speaking. I had conscientiously tried to do this last year, when I was so unhappy that I no longer recognized myself. I was at the lighthouse and every night I used to light candles as if, while they burned, they would lighten my world. I felt that I could almost see myself walking upstairs. The house was cool and dark with the sadness of late summer. I came to the three steps leading down to my room. On the last one I stopped because I was lost in the room, as in a forest at night. All I wanted was to sit down against a tree. Once long ago I fainted—I was walking down a hotel corridor when high banks of green water rose on either side of me. For a long time I walked between them and as I touched the door-handle of my room the waters closed over my head. The last thing I remembered was lying down on an ocean bed. On this night at the lighthouse I kept on walking to-wards oblivion but came instead to a table with a candlestick on it. I lighted all the candles in the room. The windows were closed and their glass reflected candles of light on the trees outside. There were ten candlesticks— two of fluted glass standing on an old blue chest, two crystal ones on a walnut table. The rest were pewter and retained rather than gave off light. I sat down and looked about the room. Then I began to realize that I saw everything in it but myself. I saw the whitewashed walls and the red floor. I saw the white rug and the pink morning-glory curtains. I saw for the thousandth time these objects and others—books and pictures and my beach pyjamas lying on the bed—but I did not yet see, even for the first time, the person sitting in the chair.

I made an effort to see this unseen person. Anyone else could see her as if she were moving on a film. I could only remember how she felt, remember certain words she said and certain things she did, but I couldn't hear her voice saying those words or see her movements as she drifted through actions which she did not know in advance she would perform. I knew—though I did not see it—that she had come and gone through this house, through a period of years, sometimes moving through a spell, sometimes through conviction and obsession, sometimes through bewilderment or outrage or despair. I was convinced that if I could actually see what she did and hear what she said I would know more about the kind of person she was and more about the trouble she was in.

I had come to believe that this kind of sight might help. Why did I believe it? Perhaps because people have tried everything else and nothing seems to have helped. No one has known human beings who give the impression of acting from knowledge of themselves or of other people. I didn't want my life to go the way of all life—to be born only to wander through experiences, to wonder at the sameness of those experiences, to want other experiences, to tire of wandering and wondering and wanting, to live at the end in remembrance of experiences, and to die—without wonder, memory, or experience.

I seemed to be doing just this, and yet I knew that in fact my life was changing. It was in this year at the lighthouse that the change began; it was in this year that the lighthouse itself changed for me. It became more than a place of peace, it will always remain for me a place where I left one of my selves which was to have no further life. I have an exact image of this separation, it left me with the feeling of being, from this time on, beside myself. The image came to me one night when I was very tired; sleep overcame me at dinner, I heard Jane's voice saying, 'Why don't you put your body down on the bed?' I remember getting up, pulling my topcoat tighter, walking a few steps to a divan and falling upon it face downwards. Hours later I wakened and went upstairs to my room. As I walked up the stairs I saw a figure in a pink topcoat on a divan. I got into my bed, I lay down. I didn't seem to be there, at least something of me wasn't there because I kept seeing myself lying face downwards, downstairs. The next morning the image persisted, it has persisted ever since—a topcoat holding a body which lay down on a bed. For me it never got up.

*Life Class*

In April we started back to Paris, where I soon found a flat in the rue Casimir Périer, with a church in front of it and a garden behind. From there we began going daily to another flat, without a garden or any other saving charm, in the rue des Colonels Renard, where Gurdjieff was living and teaching the small group I have spoken of.

I name this period the year of the predestined accident. It was in this year that I found an answer to my dilemma. The answer was that everything I had heard or experienced, at second hand—no matter how inspiring—had been too vague to produce either knowledge or understanding. The accident was that I happened to be in the right place, at the right time, in the right condition, to begin all over again.

Nothing could have been further from my preconception of what would happen to me, in this life class, than what actually began to happen. Nothing could have been further from my interpretations of what I had been told than what now appeared to take place. To me nothing took place—because what was taking place escaped me entirely.

I had always been impressed by Ouspensky's statement, in his *New Model of the Universe*, about the eternal questions, that 'people feel it is impossible, or at any rate useless, to think of these things *simply*, but what it means to think of them *not simply* they do not know.

I now expected to be plunged at once into the un-simple, which, after assimilation by my 'flashing' brain, I would understand in some unique way which I had always described as being able to understand Einstein without understanding mathematics.

Nothing like this happened. We simply went to lunch. Every day at two o'clock we gathered around a table covered with foods I had never eaten before, never even seen before. I liked them but I wasn't prepared to be interested in them. Interest was demanded; not only interest but knowledge. I found this boring, I never know what I'm eating anyway—I've had too much in-terruption in life over the quality of the butter or the preparation of the salad to be able to produce any active enthusiasm about food. I have come to the place where I eat because I'm hungry or simply because I love the ceremony of eating beautifully. The latter was incon-spicuous at the table I'm describing, and the former was honoured in a way I had never imagined. Here one ate to eat, to know what was being eaten and why. As for conversation at this table, I was bewildered by its absence and felt called upon to do more than my share in de-veloping the few remarks that were made. There were of course the toasts, and comments upon them, to which I listened lightly. After the silence of the first part of the meal, during which I was always very nervous, there was talk of a kind—formulations of great simplicity to which I gave little attention, judging that I had heard them before, in the first years at the Prieuré.

This first stage of my incomprehension lasted perhaps for two weeks, when I decided to take a more active part in the situation. Action to me has always meant rebellion, so now I began to express my disagreement with many of the things I heard. This did me no good. I watched my logic reduced to unimportance, as if logic were something that led nowhere. I had been prepared for this in theory, I wasn't at all prepared for it in fact. I fumed. This was my second phase and it lasted for months. I fumed at the table, at home during the rest of the day, and at least half the night. Sometimes I didn't sleep at all but spent the night composing all the protests I hoped and expected to make, but somehow never quite managed to, at the table. Something now always restrained me from speaking out my arguments. Instead of trying to find out what this was, I spent the time rebelling at the weakness of my resources. I had never felt weak before. Why was this stoppage upon me, how had it been imposed, why had I accepted it, why couldn't I overcome it? Months passed in this futility, my only effort being to arrive at a stronger presentation of my convictions, as well as my willingness to be convinced if only my arguments could be met and destroyed. I behaved as if I had never heard of Gurdjieff, his doctrine or its technique. No one could convince me that I was behaving this way. I thought I was kicking just enough to show that I was alive. As I saw later, it was much more than enough.

My third phase was a kind of muteness—fierce and also futile. Still understanding nothing, I still wanted to talk. But now I couldn't talk; because I couldn't be what is called 'being yourself'. I might have remembered some of those abstractions I thought I had incorporated—such as 'What sign could you give to an astute psychologist that you existed, if stripped of your five senses and your personality?' But the truth was that I could remember nothing at all—my nature was on a rampage, though it seemed to me I had never been so expressionless in my life. When Georgette and others suggested that it might be well to do nothing for a while, especially to stop running around in emotional circles, I answered in astonishment that no one had ever taken any experience more calmly, that I was in fact doing nothing at all.

I was simply trying to be myself, I said, against some force which obstructed me. I felt that if I could only talk I could make myself understood. But to talk I always needed time, a working-up of emotions before words came to me, an expenditure of gestures which helped the words to well up. Since this manifestation was barred, as the most unnecessary of all the spectacles a super-psychologist needs to watch, I increased in frenzy. My brain told me that I had been more than understood from the beginning; but my brain was proving to be (though I never recognized this truth I knew so well) merely muscular. Certainly I was demonstrating that my brain had nothing to do with *me*.

This phase lasted for perhaps a year. As it became more and more acute, as I began to despair, I realized that I was being helped by many efforts made towards me—small efforts and great ones. They helped me into a fourth phase. It was a silence—an easier silence. I no longer wished to speak. I knew by this time that I had nothing to say, that if I had lived from birth until the present moment without having spoken one word, the result would have been the same; I could simply have made gestures to show that my cup was not full but always running over. I no longer wanted to speak because I never knew what would come out. I felt like a choirboy whose voice was changing. When I thought I was going to say something in a deep calm voice to express deep appreciation, I heard myself saying the opposite in a high thin treble. During this period, which also lasted for months, I was fed with new material, little by little. I sometimes wakened in the night and found that I was sitting on the edge of my bed in the position of Rodin's 'Thinker'. But I could never remember how I got into that position or how long I had been sitting there.

During two years we went, day after day, to that same table. Day after day we were given our daily bread.

Every type at the table received the bread in a different way. No one in the group duplicated, or could really identify with, the experience of the others. Nothing could have been more divergent, for instance, than each one's attitude towards the decision of what one has to give up if one follows this 'follow-me' life. I heard Jane say that one never has to give up anything one still has a place left for. I can't know about anyone else; I had to try to give up practically everything I had made a place for, and try to give up the places as well. All my places were still there and so was my talent for filling them beautifully. I suppose I will always have those places and, if I can find the strength, will always be trying to fill them with something beyond the beautiful. One thing was apparent—no one else in the group had as much of 'the beautiful' to give up as I had. They all admitted this—some with pity, all with astonishment. Solita said she had always been unhappy, and before knowing Gurdjieff her state had become unbearable. There was no new desolation, no stripping and cleansing, no agony of effort that she didn't welcome as a change of old pain for new. This being her condition, she was led not through pain but through a new protection, combined with an effort-to-be-made which she couldn't have accepted in advance because it was one which she could never have imagined herself able to make. But she made it.

I made my effort too, but I can't be proud of it. What I feel now is that there is no shame deep enough to cover the circumstance that the effort I had to make shouldn't have been considered effort at all—and that it was almost beyond me. But this is the story of the 'doctrine'—everyman's story. This is the only testimony I can pretend to offer of a doctrine which I make no pretension of understanding in its extensions, which no one understands without being *of* it, and which it would be folly to write of in generalities. Even as I try to tell of the impact of its first dimensions I see plainly how the mystery of its extension is designed for discovery. As a baby

you learn to speak before you go to school, you employ
the mystery of language before you begin to study the
construction of the mystery.

So when I began on *a b c* it was on a parallel with my
first a b c's—I was impatient, they were unnecessary, I
already knew how to speak, why study what I could
already accomplish?

Nevertheless I began to 'study'. As a person of decision
I now found myself rushing through such rapids of in-
decision that I was always over the dam before I had
come to any decision at all. As an efficient person I was
now kept fumbling and dawdling before situations
which I could have dispatched with a turn of the wrist.
I felt that I was always standing on one foot, waiting to
put down the other foot when I was given permission,·
or when I could be sure of getting it down. I began to
hold back my whole nature for fear it wouldn't be un-
manifest enough to be invited to the table. Nothing
seemed to go right unless I felt hangdog. I used to walk
through the streets saying 'I *feel* hangdog, I *am* hangdog,
I must *be* hangdog or I'll rush in where I fear to
tread.'

As a person of order—ah, that was the straw that
broke me. At the table, as I began to recognize the order
and ceremony which propelled the doctrine's presentation, my necessity for a parallel surface order became
more obsessive than ever. I began to organize my life to
receive the doctrine. I planned. At noon I would ask a
question and hope for an answer then instead of returning for it at five o'clock, thus breaking the concentration

of my day. I would write my book in the mornings,
thus earning money to keep alive for a study of the
doctrine in the afternoons. I would keep my evenings
for a study of the sciences I had always evaded. But
morning, afternoon and evening no longer held their
positions, my relation to them was that of a wild comet
—I never knew where I might strike. And I was so dull
about this situation of chaos that I never recognized it as
order—the only order for the situation of transition.

As I began to understand the nature and purpose of
the experience I was experiencing it was easier to understand what to do. And harder to do it.

The elements of my personal universe—music, love,
nature and ideas—were slowly evolving. As for my
ideas, I saw that they might as well have been made of
paper for all the purpose they had served. As for love—
of love, art, nature—I began to know that this is not the
love which helps you to change your position.

Now that I had a speaking acquaintance with this life-
for-a-life material I tried to make a friend of it. My love
of nature and art remained to be revised. As for nature,
it had always been there, to take or to leave. But my
attitude had always been an epicurean one—I had to
take time to feast upon it beautifully. 'Oh,' I used to say
to Orage, 'I love the earth.' 'Don't talk like that,' he
said. 'Some men love the earth, as father loves child or
child father; you're only in love with it.'

I could accept this evaluation, but what could I do
about it? A day lived in nature, in my own way, had

always seemed infallible to me. . . . The rhythm of a day.
I never know a day is a day unless I live it from morning
till night in my own rhythm. It rains. I have several ways
of feeling rain fall upon my life, as if registered by a
sensitive scientific instrument. There is the first feeling—
simply, the calm rain falls; the second feeling—it falls
and I am in it, appreciating it; the third—it rains and a
conception of a day-of-falling-rain occupies me, as if I
could put it to music. If I have the day free before me
I feel that I experience rain. If I must do an errand at ten
o'clock I cannot even feel the second-depth feeling—
some flutter in me puts the experience aside, it would be
too wounding to leave it, the recording-instrument
would break.

If I can stay quiet, a day of sun is like a radio to me.
The sun tunes in, the earth rings, boats croon down the
river, I hear every sound of the day from the movement
of a leaf to the flight of a fly. THIS is a day, this is a
heavenly day, I am part of a heavenly day. My breathing
is deep and quiet, light rises and falls, a slow magnetism
flows between me and the hours.

Then there is the swift magnetism of my relation to
swiftly moving things. I know it is an adrenal rhythm
but it makes me feel as if I were a humming bee. Or a
humming motor, ready for concentrated flight. . . . I
remember a silent night when I sat in a car beside a driver
whose glands didn't move to my tempo. My adrenals
started that increasing hum. I must get my hands on the
wheel, I must, I must, a rhythm will begin, something
will release the energies of another body. I heard Solita

say, 'Do you want to drive?' She stopped the car. I got
out, got in, took the wheel. I didn't know the car, its
gears were the opposite of mine, but this didn't matter,
I needed to think to balance the vibration of feeling. My
hands touched the wheel and a contact currented between the motor's electricity and my own. Together
they established a flight. My hands lifted above the
wheel as if two electricities were running—one towards
sky, one into earth. The car and I, humming, trapezed
through the night. There was no moon—except Venus
on my left, unmoving above the rushing fields. . . .

From this life of flight, attunement, fine adjustment, I
now turned towards what I called life without nature—
animate or inanimate. My Gurdjieffian days were broken
by errands of all types—vertical lines cutting across my
horizontal plane. My days felt like barbed wire. . . . In
town, in the middle of July, walking through the nox-
ious gases of the exhaust pipes of automobiles, my throat
burning, my ears crackling with the loudspeaker city,
my head fainting with fury, my heart failing, my eyes
trying not to see what they saw but, instead, distant hills.
What's wrong with nature as an environment for man?
I shrieked to myself, from block to block. I'm an expert
in life, I have a lighthouse where all is balm and a forest
where the wind runs like water. Must I 'follow' through
this city hell? Is it necessary? Is it right? Is it good? I'm
clever enough to triumph over circumstances, why not
'help others' to find lighthouses and flats with gardens?
There's nothing left of me anyway except this cleverness,
why not put it to use? Must we all eat burning food in

a burning flat and walk the burning streets to develop a
soul?

Every day I had a new rebellion. . . . So this is the
higher life! I said. I should think that if any life could
produce authentic neurasthenia it would be just this un-
managed, mismanaged, straggling, squirming, torturing,
uninteresting, uninspired succession of days that now
present themselves to my numbed personality. I once
saw a film of a black-sheep child. She said, 'I can do what
you want if I can be boss.' So the intelligent teacher
allowed her to boss and the child's life took on direction
and inspiration. She saved herself, the school and her
parents. I have always felt like this kind of child. I felt it
now stronger than ever.

To turn my back on nature was hard enough, but to
do it to art was, I feared, beyond me. If you could know
the objective of such efforts beforehand, and their re-
vision later, you could make them more easily. And
without effect.

I had always lived on music, I wanted to hear it always, I venerated music, I think I thought that love of
music was a measure of the soul's stature. When people
told me that I knew nothing of reality I answered that
reality was my greatest enemy, that I had fought it—
successfully—all my life. My idea of what life should be
was perfectly illustrated by those pictures of Beethoven
playing to his friends, who sat listening with their heads
bowed in their hands. I was always seeking the emotion

which would allow me, compel me, to put my head in my hands. Life was never life to me unless my heart stood still.

It is like pushing aside golden clouds, trying to remember how I tried to come out from behind all this dazzlement. Even today when I suddenly hear a phrase of great lyrical music I hear myself thinking: life is music, can there be anything greater? I gather my whole organism together as if it were all needed to celebrate this glory, I listen as if listening would take me to some other sphere, I go through the complete process of hereditary build-up: is it possible I'm hearing anything so beautiful? can anything so beautiful really have been written? what did Chopin feel when he wrote it? I must arrange to hear it again right away, fortunately I can continue to hear it in memory, this is the miracle of life —that we have such memory. I felt that all people who didn't live in this state were without blessing and that they must be helped into it. I sometimes tried to decide which state—love (romantic love) or music—I could relinquish if allowed only one. For some reason I could never explain I always decided that I would have to give up love. Perhaps because one can arrange to have music continually; love isn't always available and it is so often unmusical. I played the piano under such a hypnosis of feeling that my eyes often closed under the weight of vibrations. I felt that I was accumulating more than I could use. I can't imagine, now, why this activity appeared to me like generation rather than depletion.

During 1936–8 I tried to stop living as if in emulation

of Rachmaninoff's 'Second Piano Concerto'. I entered
what I now call the D period—depression, discouragement, disgust (of self), despair, decrepitude, destruction.
Having nothing of my own left—since I no longer
wanted to live to music if I could help it—I began to
long to travel. I made lists of all the places I would go.
They always began with Innsbruck. I still wonder why.

Life now became a desert. I wouldn't musicalize and
I couldn't travel. I wouldn't have travelled if I could, all
I wanted with all my force was to get through the desert
as quickly as possible. I had better keep a record of this
new life, I said—the route between two worlds, heaven
and hell. Everything to me now is like sitting down in
the dentist's chair—the decision to sit takes all my time.
I shall have to get worse, I suppose, to get better. . . . I
drift out to dinner with another ghost-of-herself. Our
evening drops into melancholy as we sit on the terrace
of the Café Voltaire, with a moon and a wine and nothing to do or say. I look at the moon and say, 'Ah, how
lovely,' and Solita says, 'Our dead world.' The conversation stops. We walk home, I so tired of nothingness
that I begin to whistle Schumann's 'Abend', which begins on the lovely high note. I know everyone loathes
whistling but I can't resist it; then I try to be nice again
and pretend to be dazed by wine so that whatever I say
will sound irresponsible and not like the conscious speech
of a ghost. Perhaps it will sound funny and we can laugh.
But we don't laugh. We stop at the Café Bonaparte and
I say, 'Yes, let's play the slot-machine game—it's something to do, it will keep our minds off the facts.' We

both work hard to win and even now I enjoy winning or losing. . . . After the game there's nothing more to do, since I'm too tired to investigate an atom and too discouraged to study an embryo. We walk along the street and Solita says, 'Look at the moon.' I forget and say, 'Ah, how lovely' and she says 'Our dead world.' By the time I reach home I'm groggy with non-existence. But Georgette is there to laugh at me and predict that tomorrow will be better. I laugh hysterically and take courage. But as Emma Goldman used to say, 'What has this got to do with the revolution?' What has this got to do with the riddle of the universe which was my only reason for starting on this quest?

Things got better, and then worse again. If I have anything to say I might as well say it in that phrase— better then worse then better then worse.

The worst, the very worst, had to do with people. 'Something is terribly wrong,' I said, 'either with me or with them, when people whom I know to be completely unversed in life seem to get on more intelligently with this new life than I do.' Since they did, how could I trust the new life? People whose perceptions seemed to me so blunted that I wouldn't trust them to detect the difference between a horse and a cow in a field—how was it that they seemed to understand the meaning of this doctrine better than I did? I had always rejected such people in life—they knew none of the things I knew; now I saw them outstripping me and I couldn't stand it. What were they perceiving that I wasn't? What was the value of the thing perceived since their perceptions were of such a crude nature? But I didn't hate these people, I envied them; I didn't grow bitter, I simply admitted that I was stupider than they. This attitude was the only quality I showed that I didn't have to be ashamed of afterwards.

The next phase was nausea. . . . I woke in the morning feeling seasick. Nothing to do, that I *could* do, made me bilious. I felt that I was deep yellow, I hated everything I loved. All my life I've had experience with physical nausea; in the long period that precedes release I pass through a list of rejections of all that I love and now hate —pianos, trees, ideas. Now I felt deep yellow in an environment of deep black. If I could only go back to feeling 'normal' and work at something—houses, plans, piano, book—what HAVE I worked at so hard (easily) all my life? WHAT plans? I can't remember. WHAT was I working at? One would have thought, at least, the Golden Gate bridge.

I now evaluated all my much-ado-about-something as nothing. I had nothing that I could respect. I even began to hate my face-expression. I may have been a darling of the gods—that was my trouble. I saw no good in the face-expression of a darling. I wished that I might have begun this experience far beyond the status of a darling. Still, I now understood enough to know that it doesn't matter where you begin, the thing is to begin; advantages are always offset by disadvantages, everyone starts equal before a unique activity.

# A Life for a Life

To understand—that was the necessity. Understand your nature and the nature of your type. All the qualities which had composed 'our' superiority now emerged as unrelated to that need of being born again. Our imaginations had been the excess of desire over ability. Our intelligence had been merely a justification of this excess. Our intense emotions had amounted to the pleasure of having emotions. Our art had been a hope of repeating those emotions for ever. Our 'rich' personalities had been an obstacle to understanding these facts. We who had been born outside the dull, the routine, the conflicting; we the convinced, the convincing; we the inspired, the inspiring—what had we been all our lives? Almost nothing at all. We were balloons that had got up to the ceiling and stayed there because we couldn't get any higher. We had considered ourselves Nietzchean transvaluers of all values, but all we had really done was to act like Gabriele D'Annunzio.

Georgette as usual had a picture of our plight. 'We have spent our lives walking about under parasols,' she said. Yes, I thought—white silk parasols, like those used by Catholics in midnight Mass at New Year's.

From now on I had a more concrete picture of the soft past and the hard future. Each period always seemed an end and always proved to be only a beginning. To the end of life, I suppose, this will be my condition of life. There was the abstract period, the stable-cleaning period, the camel-through-the-needle's-eye period, the rat-on-the-wheel period—the impulse, the decision, the effort, the work, the fluctuation, the rebellion, the recession, the new decision, the new effort. I now saw that if you can manage to qualify, something will be revealed to you. The more you can qualify the more you will be invited to qualify. This will go on until the rat-on-the-wheel situation has attained its zenith. Then if it's in you to keep on turning, you stay on the wheel. But the wheel is not merely the wheel of life, nor is it Ouspensky's New Model of the Universe. It is another formula.

It had taken me a long time to find out what I was finding out day by day. It had been a long time since I had remembered my life year after year. My years were no longer chronological or pictorial, they were not a passage of time but a passage from one accretion to another. A year was now worth no more than its formulations. I no longer said 'Remember the year when we first heard Stravinsky's "Sacre"?' or 'That was the year of the nightingale.' I now said, 'Remember the year when I was told "You rest in dream"?' These four words—so simple, said so long ago—are the only direct words of Gurdjieff to me that I have quoted in this book.

And I remember the year when I could at last formulate 'I am empty.' I remember my first horror and incredulity as I screamed (to myself) '*I* empty? I who have always been so interested in the nature of the universe?'

Then I remember the day when, suddenly, I had no more screaming to do, only cracking. There were guests for lunch that day, at Gurdjieff's table. Among them was one from the old days at the Prieuré, one who should have known from the beginning that 'Gurdjieff is not a single man but a multitude, and through the multitude there walks a sage; in his talk there is always teaching; you must watch for it, you must not be put off.' This woman appeared not to know it, or not to want to know, or not to want to show that she knew. I may misjudge her, but I could only believe that she didn't know. And when she said, 'Good heavens, the same old repertoire, I don't see how you stand it day after day,' I felt that she didn't even suspect what was taking place. In the repertoire that day, when none of the guests seemed to be listening, six words were said to me—placed formally in the informal talk. After lunch the unsuspecting guest said, 'Was that a special crack you got?' 'Oh no,' I said. One of the less unsuspecting said, 'Don't take it too hard, whatever it was.' 'Oh no,' I said, 'it was just a hint.'

It had been a revelation. For the first time I knew that my shell had cracked open. For the first time I saw that I was as stupid as I was vain, and as egotistic as I was empty.

It was afternoon when the lighthouse emerged for us, again, from its trees and the river. The tide was high, birds were singing, flowers blooming, the sun and air and earth received us again for another summer.

Inside I looked once more at the rooster plates, and the cracked ones with roses. Ten years had passed since we first came here and everything was the same. I walked up the spiral stairs. I walked down the three steps to my room and opened the windows. Air from the forest entered. I sat down. Everything was the same. But I was not.

I had always been the same before, no matter what had happened to me or in me or around me. What could I say to anyone who asked me what change was, or why I was changed, or what I thought had changed in me? I tried to formulate the hair's-breadth difference which would contain the meaning. I would say = I now have something which no page of philosophy, psychology, cosmology, physics, chemistry, geology, biology, astronomy, astrology, microscopy, mathematics, metaphysics, magic or mysticism could have given me. They would say = But the Bible? No, I would say, no page of Bible. They would say = What can Gurdjieff give that the Bible doesn't give? I would say = Everything. The Bible doesn't give it, only shows it. No words on paper can give you anything except what you yourself make them give. You can't make them give enough. You can make them give you a faith. That is a great deal. It is not enough, since there is something more.

I could hear the voices of millions of preachers sending out their Sunday words over radios—'Have faith.' I suddenly heard Bach composing 'I call upon Thee, Jesus'— because he *had* faith. I suddenly heard a simple man telling of the white light that shines for him around the words 'Do unto others as you would have others do unto you.' I remembered all the voices from my past. 'Can't you just accept the fact that there is Something and stop worrying?' 'No,' I always said. 'Can't you

126

accept an hypothesis, as a scientist does, and go along with it until it gives out?' 'No,' I said. 'Why not?' 'Why should I? We already know where all the hypotheses have given out.' 'Can't you just have faith in God and rest on that?' 'No,' I said.

Faith in God. You understand what faith is, you try to understand what God is. I thought about the St. Paul type of faith—that conviction of faith in faith. I thought about another type of faith—that conviction of the unknown knowable. I wondered how this faith could be put into words on paper. I would begin by stating the subject. The subject is: the nature of the human soul and its fate—without, or with, cultivation. If I were allowed only a few sentences to develop such a subject, I would choose a summary once made by Solita: 'There is a force in man which natural man does not develop. This force, known to Hermetic science, is the "life of men"—the essence of that mystical vine of which we are the branches—without which there could be no consciousness at all. Humanity unaided can never find this secret, it must be initiated into the supernatural principle which man has within him, which scientifically is called the "life principle" without the scientists or religionists suspecting what it is they call "life". The real religion communicates only two commands to the world, over and over, for the few who wish to be chosen—"As above so below" and "You must be born again". For rebirth there is an exact science, the greatest in the world and sacredly concealed. Why? If it were told what would become of the law: Seek and you will find?'

## A Life for a Life

I went on thinking of how this knowledge can be learned, of the conditions in which it can be communicated, of the method of its communication: no information that goes into the mind alone; no stimulation for the mind which will merely leave you satisfied with stimulation; no stimulation for your feelings which will leave you content merely to feel; no rewards for the personality; no great revelations—until they take place. And on your part: no mere taking thought; no withdrawal from the world; no sacrifices too great to make —once you have made them; no impasses of time, or money, or need to earn your daily bread—they must be or will be or can be resolved. And if you don't find a Gurdjieff? You do—if you search.

I saw the evolution of man in a new picture—as long as a million years of the evolution of a universe. I saw every phenomenon turning on that hair's-breadth difference which becomes—creation. I saw a long cord from womb to womb, and another from 'self' to 'self'.

I saw myself—no longer sitting on a cloud; nor was I left sitting on the ground. I was no longer unhappy, nor would I be happy again. I would never again be anything but rejoicing. A blessing was upon me, I felt it on every side. I would no longer be spared, or killed, or protected. I would be helped. Years will pass and I know what I will be doing. I do not know where I will live, what I will eat or wear, how I will look or 'feel', or whom I shall be seeing. In the world there will be war, in my world there will be no peace—except that which passes understanding: a lifetime for a life—for 'what

128

abides shining, not burning, as below, or wrathful; but vital, calm, transmuting, recreating, and no longer a consuming fire'.

*Paris, March*, 1938.

## VI

# AN EFFORT THAT FAILED?

WHEN THE manuscript of *The Fiery Foun-tains* was finished I waited optimistically for an eager publisher, convinced that the Gurdjieff part would impress him. But months went by and no one wanted it; two years passed, and every first-rate publishing-house in America said 'This is a book that could never sell'.

Jane, who was in London, gave the manuscript to our old friend and *Little Review* contributor, T. S. Eliot, hoping that Faber and Faber would want it. But Eliot too refused, and gave his reasons:

Dear Jane—well, what on earth am I to do about Margaret's book? It is certainly very readable; it is certainly very egocentric; and it certainly bears out all of the impression that you gave me of Margaret and her relation to the Gurdjieff activities. But would it interest anybody who was not already interested in Margaret? I cannot believe that it would catch an immediate public, and I cannot believe that its future for another generation is one worth investing in. So the only thing to do is to return it to you, with the remark that I very much enjoyed reading it. And is there anything else I can do about it, or that you would like me to do about it?

I wrote to Eliot: 'If you enjoyed reading my book, why won't others? And how on earth can you believe that Djuna Barnes's *Night Wood*, which you published with such excessive praise, has any significance for future generations? Its only virtue is that Djuna knows how to write. For what *enlightenment* can future generations turn to her book? But then neither can they turn to your Church of England, which holds no enlightenment for mankind. Gurdjieff's doctrine does.'

I didn't send the letter. Useless to defend one's faith when it involves a conflict with conventional religion.

Finally, seven years later, *The Fiery Fountains* was accepted by Gorham Munson. He was then head of a new firm (since dissolved) called Hermitage House, and he took the book because he was a literary man, because he had known both Gurdjieff and Orage, and because he was glad I had written about them.

All the critics (with two or three exceptions)

praised *The Fiery Fountains* as 'a book of supreme interest', 'a feat of outstanding communication', 'the story of a woman engaged in the higher art of living', 'a flaming spirit', etc., which of course pleased me, but no one wrote about the Gurdjieff part. Finally a cynical friend—a publisher's reader —explained why. 'Many reviewers', she wrote, 'have given your book the "go-by", or silent treatment, because they realized they couldn't either cope with, or afford to ignore, its most important part—the Gurdjieff.'

I was amused by a card from Edmund Wilson: 'I have done a little note on your book for the *New Yorker*, but I am sorry I couldn't give a more exciting account of it, because all that Gurdjieff business depresses me. What I liked best in it was the directions for romantic love.'

The little note never appeared. I wondered why. But most of all I wondered why Wilson wasn't depressed by all that Dead Sea Scrolls business.

At last, from London, came a letter from John Bennett, whom I had met in Gurdjieff's Paris flat in 1948. It was his criticism of what I *hadn't* managed to do that interested me most:

'A remarkable achievement', he wrote—'book that deserves to be a classic in its genre. The great difficulty is that any picture of Gurdjieff must of necessity be one-sided and incomplete. No one could know Gurdjieff, and of necessity each person saw him with the eyes that he or she had open. One thing that no one must do is to write an imaginary story of the "real Gurdjieff", which they cannot know. This you have rightly avoided.

'I will be quite out-spoken and say exactly as I think. What you have written about Gurdjieff is sincere and modest. You have not tried to represent yourself as having a privileged position, or being somehow in possession of secrets which are denied to other people. This is how it should be, and you have a right to be pleased. Many people will be grateful to you. At the same time, you have constantly missed things by your very eagerness to find them. Your ardour for the ideal has often prevented you from seeing the significance of the actual. Seeing yourself as a crusader for truth, you did not see that Gurdjieff himself was fighting for another Truth on a scale beyond your imagining.

'I write this because the only specific criticism that I would make of your book is that you do not sufficiently convey the "unknowableness" of Gurdjieff. I do not suggest that this could have been done easily. Any kind of "mystery-mongering" would strike a completely false note, and this you have most rightly avoided. I have in mind rather a matter-of-fact *avertissement* to the reader that Gurdjieff was and has remained unknowable, so that each person who met him could discover little more than a reflection of himself.

'You will understand that I am making this criticism

only because I take your book very seriously and regard it as an important contribution to the great work of preparing for the entry of Gurdjieff's ideas into the life of mankind.'

I'm not sure that Bennett ever realized how much I appreciated, and agreed with, his view of my failure. But where is the mental giant who can convey Gurdjieff's unknowableness, and to what audience shall he convey it? Or, since the unknowable cannot be conveyed, why study what cannot be known? Or, if the unknowable is what ultimately becomes known, as in the natural sciences, where is the inspired disciple who will ultimately reveal it, now that Gurdjieff is dead? The intellectuals and religionists, who should be the first to recognize his mystery and profit by his illuminations, have offered nothing but total incomprehension.

## A SECOND FAILURE

I gave the manuscript of this present book to Solita, to read and criticize, and she wrote to me as follows:

'The title of your book is misleading. You do not speak of any knowable or unknowable Gurdjieff, really. You have not indicated the most important aspects of Gurdjieff or made a reader feel

his mysterious knowledge or X-ray insight. No
matter what you may reply to this that I say, *you
have not done it*, not even by long-distance osmosis.
It could have been done and I think you should
have done it—though perhaps you could not easily
have discovered the way. But you did not. You
should have given some indication of Gurdjieff's
status and scope as a great initiate. This would have
given your book another flavour and *raison d'être*,
and also a reference-point like the magnet of the
North Pole, to what followed.

'Your "Life for a Life" chapter is very fine. But
for the rest, and for such a title, it is not enough
to give, through other people, a *sense* of his
mystery. You could have had an adequate title, an
indication of his teaching and mystery as "understood" and felt through them.'

To which I replied: 'I can only agree with you,
though I did feel that I had given (even vaguely)
some sense of his scope and mystery, and that my
quotations from others contributed largely to such
an evaluation. Why don't *you* write a passage indicating your againstment and *your* conception of
his "status and scope"?'

Solita answered: 'I cannot now. Six months
would be too short a time.'

'Then you must write a book yourself. But this
you will refuse to do.'

# VII

# CETTE AUTRE CHOSE

GEORGETTE'S EFFORT to incorporate what she had assimilated during her years with Gurdjieff is recorded in the last part of her book, *La Machine à Courage*. The French press hailed the book as a chef-d'œuvre, and Cocteau did a preface for it, but no American publisher could be persuaded to take it. Therefore I include its final chapters here:

*Fontainebleau-Avon, France*

... It was in June, 1924, that Margaret, Jane and I went to stay at the Château du Prieuré, for it was there that Gurdjieff lived and received people who sought him out from all over the world.

My impression of Gurdjieff was that he resided on the earth as on a planet too limited for his own needs and function. Where did he manifest his real existence? In his teaching, in his writings, not at all in ordinary social life which he seemed to regard as a vast *blague* and manipulated with resignation or impatience.

I was not astonished that he was little known, that he was not surrounded by thousands of followers. Neither money nor influence could open the doors of the Prieuré—Gurdjieff created all possible obstacles to discourage any idler-spirits who might push their way into a world where they did not belong.

I have never been able to acclimatize myself to esoteric cults and doctrines with their vague followers—instinctively I turn away. On the contrary, the sharp climate of Gurdjieff's mentation held me. It was a difficult climate; to live in it one had to possess an invincible need.

To know something of the stature of the man one had to listen to the reading of his manuscript—an enormous work in nine parts. My silent listening disappointed many in the audience who expected some audible sign of my interest; but I was entirely occupied in the process of absorbing, like a plant that has waited for water all its life.

'I cannot develop you', Gurdjieff told us, 'I can create conditions in which you can develop yourselves.'

Those conditions were hard, yet my greatest distress was not to have known earlier this hard instruction. In the beginning it seemed heartbreaking to approach such truths at last and to have so few years left to give to them. But soon the fact that I was working within myself, with an unawakened part of my nature, supplied me with a new strange energy. From now on I would know how to use the time remaining to me—I pictured myself as a honeycomb with each cell waiting to be filled.

I followed avidly the daily monastic life of the Prieuré

—the conversations, the readings, the communal work in the gardens. Each day I tried to foresee the stages through which I would pass and I laughed at myself, at this poor human being who dared to say: 'I want "to be", I dedicate my life to this end.' It was like saying, 'I shall work to fly like a bird'. A scale runs from tadpole to bird, and I did not know the number of notes. I knew only that each note led to the next and that nothing in the world—book, word or prophesy—would help me to know in advance what the next one would be. It would depend essentially on my organism.

What astonished me was not to understand a little, but to see that some people—newcomers to the Prieuré—did not understand at all. I sometimes had flashes of 'consciousness' so strong that a heat invaded me. Every hour I became aware of a soul I had not nurtured.

Two stories for each individual . . . himself and his shadow (that is, his 'soul'). His appearance comes and goes with a name, a situation; his shadow—a reality which exists only by virtue of light—awaits its hour and enters *en seène* only at the end. I saw myself, like all human beings, as a repetition-machine; and I had always aspired to a different state. Too long now I had rested in that illusory 'I' that is like a Chinese *magot* whose head nods 'yes' perpetually to all our blindnesses, perpetually approves all our acts. Now I wanted to finish with all that old automatic life, so pleasant but so null—human life which leads to nothing unless it leads to everything. I began to work to change, and I felt as if I were being torn from my roots. Why should I cling so hard to that which I no longer clung to, which I had never really clung to. Did I underestimate the power of the bonds which attached me to . . . nothing? Yes. I had thought myself different from my parents because I had lived my life differently. But what essential difference is there in that? It is only the menu of days, like the menu of meals.

I am always asked, in respect of this cosmogony which has now held my attention for so many years, 'Is your source the same as Katherine Mansfield's?' I answer, 'Yes, in fact; no, in essence.'

In her *Journal* Katherine Mansfield wrote of the last months of her life at the Prieuré. It is not known that Gurdjieff had admitted her to his Institute with a reservation (to his intimates): that it was too late to help her physically, but possible to help her in other ways.

It is of these 'other ways' that her Journal and Letters record less than she was able to express in her conversations with Orage. The greatness of Katherine was her sincerity. She was not pious, yet she felt the need of a redemption, of a system of 'purity'. She wanted a spiritual life stripped of the clichés of religion. This spirituality of which she had such a magnificent need can be had without recourse to Gurdjieff—it already exists in the best of religion. It can be had without great effort. Gurdjieff offers much more. He is not consoling; he is better than that. What he offers is hard, like the teaching of Jesus—if one gets to its source. There is no Truth that is *complaisante*. I think that the first requisite for an approach to Gurdjieff is a condition of health; one must be

in full force to support the first shocks. There is, to begin
with, the inconceivable torment of feeling oneself a
ground that is being ploughed up. All at once our forces
are solicitated for an unknown labour. It is impossible.
The more one sees and understands the more one thinks
'I cannot'. But is it our forces that are solicitated? No. It
is a question of forces that we have never used, that we
are ignorant of . . . new energies awakened by a new
need, towards a new goal.

Although at the Prieuré I experienced a happiness
beyond any I had ever known, I also fell from despair to
despair. My anxiety was total, I lived the meaning of the
word '*boulversée*'. At each instant I touched the depths of
my distress—a vague distress in which I did not entirely
participate. Even when a new flash of understanding
came to me I felt more lost than ever. The essential that
I was seeking remained hidden from my sight. My only
hope of finding it lay in my capacity for effort.

'But why do you want this knowledge?' my old
friends asked. Strange question. No one asks 'Why do
you want happiness?' To me knowledge—or rather, understanding—is a perfect synonym for happiness. Others
said, 'Never look inside yourself, it is fatal'; or, 'What
can one do with one's life when one has lost all illusions?'
I answered, 'That's as if a farmer said, "All the weeds in
my fields have been pulled up, what can I do with the
ground now?" '

Years and years ago I used to think: 'Our natures
should be ploughed up as the ground is ploughed.' But

where was the plough, and who would guide it? Alone we could do nothing. The plough and the planter were as necessary as the seed.

Gurdjieff's 'method' indicated the instrument and the guide. They were ready and waiting; it was for me to be ready and willing. Wish, need, and effort—it was with these requirements that one approached that 'other life' with its special efforts, its new laws, its different evolution which tended to change even the chemistry of one's organism. It was to be a difficult life. At the Prieuré I watched certain people stop half-way, renounce or branch off, become enemies and enrol themselves in some promising system which guaranteed paradise at the end of their days. Sometimes they returned to religion and declared themselves 'touched by grace'—a grace which usually corresponded to their most material needs and in which they installed themselves comfortably, with all their luggage, as if for a voyage. They took a one-way ticket to paradise, but I noticed that more often than not they changed it for a round-trip.

What an error it is to believe that suffering alone is enough for self-development. If it were, our planet would already be covered with saints and angels. Suffering kills some people; others are deformed by it; some become mad; only a few improve or progress. One must have more knowledge to benefit by suffering.

All my life I had instinctively been a believer, but I could not accept the God proposed by religion . . . a God conceived merely as a refuge or a hope, when He should be the divine progression of the soul which contains

Him. But every human being is the mirror of the God he conceives, and most are pocket-mirrors.

During all my first months at the Prieuré my ground was being ploughed. For a long time I thought I had recognized my nonentity; for a long time I thought I had known my vanity. Now I saw that this judgment was still a kind of vanity. So I watched myself, I began to know myself a little.

For two years we lived at intervals at the Prieuré. From then on until 1935 we encountered Gurdjieff more rarely, but we continued to live, as far as we could, according to his principles, absorbing his doctrine more and more deeply.

. . . When people reach my age they announce in a tone of curious satisfaction that they are getting old, their task is done, they can now relax, it is for others to live. They judge life to be finished when to me it has barely begun. They see it as a curve, when it can and should be an ascending line. To me, life begins at fifty and never stops growing. It is the moment to live '*autre chose*'.

I have the feeling that I have lived all my life for my particular present. I must admit that I have not finished with art and moonlight, music and spring, and that I will never be insensible to all the delights that are the adorable froth of the earth. But these delights are now no longer between my sight and my life. Learning to 'live' demands no startling abdications. It leaves old delights their place, but not their ancient power; it brings a new purpose, a new fire, and infinite new ways of seeing all things.

. . . The material of my former life now lay behind me. It was my first life, the life none of us knows how to live—except in disorder and bewilderment. I was now ready to give all my energy to those conditions which Gurdjieff had named as the terms of development. It was not easy. I felt like a bird tapping to get out of its shell. What lay beyond, for me, would be as different as the world outside the shell would be for the bird.

Often I wanted to escape, to turn away from this super-science which demanded too much of me. Yet escape seemed criminal, as well as impossible. A truth once perceived, even for a second, is never lost; it comes to light again in spite of everything. And if one wants to live this truth, one realizes that one has been promised to it, that all the events of a lifetime have been converging towards it.

I was slowly changing, and I was afraid of no longer recognizing myself. Between the non-existent image which had been my companion and this new image that I barely saw, a fog was rising. In it both images were obliterated and I pursued them blindly, afraid of finding neither.

. . . The year 1936 arrived. I had surmounted three grave illnesses in the past four years, but I had not yet regained my familiar endless energies.

During my struggle with death I had thought, 'If I am

to live, I swear to myself to go further than before . . . I do not give myself the right to come out of danger in the same state in which I entered it.'

Later, as danger withdrew, all the useless associations, the superfluous speculations, returned. I was saved, but restored to habit—to all that we call normal life. . . . And I was accepting it!

A cry of revulsion rose in me, rested petrified in my throat. I sensed that a new cycle of catastrophes would begin if I could not, by a supreme effort, turn my life at last towards its high aim. I must begin to understand better what I already understood, all that the past had taught me in showing me that what is essential lies elsewhere.

This life of mine which in the past had seemed beautiful—had none of it served a purpose? This perfumed wax in which I had modelled my years of art, of love, and faith in both—was this all that I could contribute to the miracle of a life on earth? No, no, I was ready to step from the present into what would be, at last, the future—that future which is in us and awaits our attention.

*A Well of Water*

'But whosoever drinketh of the water that I shall give him shall never thirst; but the water that I shall give him shall be in him a well of water springing up into everlasting life.'—*St. John* 4, 14

And so, armed with a supreme resolution, I arrived at

that moment of life which is called descending the other side of the hill, but which to me is an ascension.

Gurdjieff was again in Paris and I was able to see him continually until the war began in 1939. Of that constant association with him, of that work towards 'development' which no well-being, no happiness, could equal for me, I find it almost impossible to write.

Many people have investigated doctrines analogous to the Gurdjieff science. To write of them in a word, in a few words, in infinite words, is to deform them—the truth that can enter into a formula is limited. To write abstractly of Gurdjieff's conceptions in relation to other great systems of thought, belief, religion, is equally futile. I know the danger of verbalizing over abstract ideas—unless it is to repudiate them. Negations are greeted kindly, and the thinker who offers nothing but an hypothesis is always respected. An hypothesis is a life-belt for the mind; thanks to it, the mind floats a little longer before sinking.

I know, too, what the very term 'search for truth' suggests of the absurd, the pretentious, the erroneous, the hysterical. Research seems futile. It is less so, however, than to settle one's self comfortably, eyes closed, into a life of which one understands nothing.

And so, in relation to Gurdjieff's doctrine, which became for me 'truth', I shall tell simply what I have felt, experienced and understood. I shall not say what I hope from it, but what I have learned to want from it. I shall try to tell what it has done for me in transforming my aspirations into a single and total energy.

# Cette Autre Chose

In the little red diary which lies before me on my desk I reread the record of what I felt, experienced and understood during those three great years. I live again the exaltation and the agony of those daily efforts I made to awaken and develop what was sleeping in me, as in all human beings.

I have copied out some pages of this diary—words written from time to time in the long nights without sleep which became for me my nights of light.

## DIARY

*Paris, June, 1936.* Apartment finally found, rue Casimir Perier, between the church and trees.

Often in pain. Difficult epoch, but marvellous end of month because of my new meeting with Gurdjieff. Went to see him in the café where he always sits before lunch.

'Time passes for me', I said to him, 'and I make no progress. I have not many more years to live; will you allow me to read the new parts of your manuscript?'

He looked long at me. At last he said, 'You still have time to live. Yes, come to lunch tomorrow and you will read.' He murmured words I did not understand. Finally I caught, 'You are young, but liver sick, all organs blocked.' He paused and then said, 'Yes, I will do for you.' I wanted to cry out my gratitude but I restrained myself, knowing that he understood all I felt. I articulated painfully, 'Thank you.'

*June 22.* Lunched with him, his family and a few pupils in his apartment. After lunch he showed me a little room and a cupboard where he would leave his manuscript for me. He said I might come and read whenever I liked.

*June 27.* Every day I spend two or three hours at his flat. I read with concentration, as if my life depended on the difficult thought that comes from his pages.

*June 28.* Ill again. Couldn't go to read.

*June 30.* Last night had an acute crisis of pain which involved all the nerves of the solar plexus.* But I shall go to read to-morrow.

*Thursday, July 16.* I am much better. Told Gurdjieff that for the first time in twenty years I have slept the night through. He was glad, and not surprised. He assured me that I would recover, that he had a plan for me, and repeated a second time, 'You are young.' I understood later that he was referring to my healthy glands. He explained that the first part of the work would take five years, that the body must be strong enough to march with the spirit, because the world of the spirit depends on the body which carries it. In Thibet, where he spent so many years of his life, the priests are doctors and the doctors priests.

At lunch he told the others that my case interested him—'She was candidate for death, she is already candidate for life.' Then he looked at them with eyes of mischief. 'I only said to her, "Read the book, madame, read the book".'

*July 20.* What physical amazement when I find I can lie full length on my bed, after so many years of half-reclining; and what astonishment in a body that is dreading pain which does not come. I often feel a great internal heat, as if I were close to a fire. I sleep without waking. I believe that a silent and healing perturbation is taking place in me. I understand what is happening, but to *live* it is unbelievable.

*July 27.* Arrived at his flat tired, dragging myself along. Read

* This was the last attack.

the book for three hours. When I left I felt light and strong. Walked two kilomètres without weariness. Physically I am living a springtime in this cold month of July. I feel charged like a dynamo.

*July 30.* Gurdjieff came in while I was reading. I was at the end of the chapter on religions. Told him my exaltation in as few words as possible—he doesn't like 'manifestations'. He was visibly satisfied.

He considers that my health is better and better. As I was leaving he said, 'As yet nothing. Soon will begin something more.'

*End of August.* Never any more pain. I discern something immense that is happening in me. Evidently the brain is not our sole organ of control—other organs also register what takes place in us, and perhaps more accurately than the brain does. I have the impression of a wheel turning within me, motored by a renewed bloodstream and by my conscious will to receive the help given me. I am experiencing the wonderment of something that is not hereditary.

*September 27.* For several months it has been clear that men are unconsciously creating what they call the inevitable—that is, war; and at the same time declaring sincerely that they want only peace.

*September 30.* Every day I go to study his manuscript. I consider it the authentic event of my life.

The time of destruction—the war—approaches. Yet we work to finish our apartment, which is more and more adorable because of the arched doorways we have constructed throughout. Sooner or later we will lose it.

I have a special anguish as I realize the strength of the

energies restored to me. Desires, needs, wishes now assail me, after three years in which I have tried to reconcile myself to the idea of death.

*October 29.* Another period of dark days. Since I am no longer tense with perpetual suffering, I feel a curious laxness. And then winter is on the way. My organism follows the uneasiness of the earth beneath its pale cold colours. The branches of trees make mechanical gestures towards the sky. One's organism has its habits. Because mine has suffered so long it wants to go on suffering. It is more nervous, more sensitive. And I feel myself slipping, I have moments of discouragement. I try not to admit them but they are there nevertheless.

*October 31.* I described my state to him. He already knew and his words brought me comfort, for he made me understand how the law of up-and-down works in all functioning.

*Monday, the 2nd of November.* A great emotion today. When I arrived at Gurdjieff's apartment it was he himself who opened the door. I said immediately, 'I am completely well, I am in a new body.' The light that came from the little salon illuminated him fully. Instead of avoiding it, he stepped back and leaned against the wall. Then, for the first time, he let me see what he really is . . . as if he had torn off the masks behind which he is obliged to hide himself. His face was stamped with a charity that embraced the whole world. Transfixed, standing before him, I saw him with all my strength and I experienced a gratitude so deep, so sad, that he felt a need to calm me. With an unforgettable look he said, 'God helps me.'

*November 4.* From the beginning he has said, 'I can prevent pain and thereby prepare the ground for something else.' I know that he means a special work, in which the tempo of the spirit will keep pace with the physical recovery. But have I the strength to undertake it?

*November 25.* Tonight after dinner Gurdjieff played his little accordion-piano. Unique spectacle. This is the man who says, 'I try to be a man without quotation marks.' As he played one saw a man live—as complete as a circle. And the richness of his smile! Richness of bounty, richness of truth.

*Christmas Eve, 1936.* Extraordinary reunion at his flat tonight. Another age—a patriarch distributing treasures. The little apartment was full—his family, friends of his family, the concierge and his family, old servants from other days. The Christmas tree, too big, too high, was bent against the ceiling and its stars hung down.

The distribution of gifts was a true ceremony. Fifty or more large boxes, numbered, occupied a corner of the salon. Gurdjieff, standing in front of a table, glasses on his nose, held a list in his hand. To each box that was set before him he added notes of a hundred or five hundred francs; then he called a name corresponding to a number and presented the box, making the brief gesture that signifies 'Don't thank me.' The last to come forward was a Danish doctor who received a handsome dressing-gown and a thousand-franc note. As Gurdjieff placed the money in the box S. said, 'He's going to be happy, that one.' Gurdjieff answered like lightning, 'Not you?'

At ten o'clock supper was served. On each plate was an enormous piece of mutton, a stuffed Russian roll, pickles, peppers preserved in oil—all the things I hold in horror; but superb desserts were spread out—cakes, fruits, candies of a thousand-and-one nights. We left at midnight and other people took our places. The Russian maid said to me, 'From one o'clock till dawn the poor will be coming.'

# Cette Autre Chose

We know that for him a period of fasting will follow this feast, to balance so many days of abundance.

*December 30.* Resurrection ... absorbing and primordial question for me—the successive deaths and the perpetual renewals of life: addition of what was, what is, and what will be. A new kind of resurrection begins in me—I am invaded by the all-powerfulness of spirit. This surpasses life itself.

*December 31.* If I am able to understand Gurdjieff a little in his entirety, it is because I have studied him and his doctrine for over twelve years. One of his greatest values is knowing how to render intelligible to human understanding the truths that are the most impossible for the mind of man to conceive.

My intelligence—no, I don't value it; and anyway, in these matters, intelligence moves into second place. What I have always valued in myself is not my intelligence but a fundamental lucidity which has never failed me in all the disasters of my existence. Before my experience with Gurdjieff I saw the time approaching when this lucidity alone would be left in me, like a flag on an empty house.

My notes from January, 1937, to the following December show only long months of effort—the climbing and falling known to all those who have tried to follow the difficult 'road of knowledge'.

But what does this vague phrase, road of knowledge, mean? Philosophers claim that all knowledge can be found within four walls, in books. Yet everyone can read Hermès, Pythagoras, Buddah, the Bible, and remain blind before these closed codes. It is not enough to read, admire, speculate. The study of 'Know thyself' demands a special work and a life given up to it. One must begin the work. What one has learned, one must incorporate. The time that stretches between these two states is full of panic. But all initiation holds a period of panic, just as all work holds within it the same laws: the road which at first appears to be vertical becomes less steep as one climbs.

Some of the pages of my diary during this period are almost incoherent with despair. At other moments I had no despair, neither had I hope. I was living in a tunnel. Then on the tenth of October I wrote:

I know that I am approaching a momentous state. I know the balance I must maintain in all the coming tests, and some lines of Goethe haunt me: 'No path! It is the jungle that one cannot penetrate . . . And then in the eternally empty distance you will see nothing, you will not hear the sound of your footsteps, you will have nothing upon which to rest. . . .'

I know this and I detest my anguish. However great it is I judge it to be small. Yet I am afraid—with a thousand fears which have 1.o name. It is my parents, my ancestors, who are afraid in me. Why listen to their fears? I was not so afraid when I faced death. Was that, then, more natural? Yes.

Others before me have done what I am doing. But that does not help me—each person's experience is different. I envy those who plunge in without hesitating. I am ashamed of my hesitation, I seem to be bargaining. A small life for a great truth—I must choose. Yet I want to discuss the choice with myself before I give up this self to its task. I will advance in darkness; 'seeing' will be abolished for the sake of 'being'. The hardest moment of all will arrive. The guide will watch me stumble, exhaust myself, and will say nothing. His words were:

'I cannot develop you, I can create the conditions in which you can develop yourself.'

*October 12.* I had a dream. I walked for years, searching a planet. Across space I arrived. At first I thought that the cities, the people, the things, were like ours. Soon I saw that all was different. People loved one another and they did not speak. The animals spoke.

I had a long conversation with a white horse as large as a cathedral. He explained to me his two-dimensional vision and his terrors. He understood that I was burning and to relieve me he hung his mane like a rain about my body. It was he who explained the celebration of a fête such as does not exist in our world. Three seasons had conquered the fourth. I watched the triumphal return of the troops—regiments of all the countries advanced, flags flying, followed by springtime and early autumns. They had killed the winters.

They were not accompanied by good and evil. Their songs were bells, their laughter was like the sunlit sea. To amuse themselves along the way they had disciplined plagues, abolished pain, hunted down calumny. My companion said, 'With winter dead, they have killed the inevitable. Now death will be no more than a result—the consequence of not having understood.'

Suddenly one of the men fell from high up on to the ground before me. He split in two. He was empty.

*October 18.* The important moment is here, my choice has been made. Tomorrow we will ask Gurdjieff—Margaret and I—whether the time has come for us to begin our real work.

When I really begin, nothing will have changed in appearance. I will still have my name that I do not like, I will be dressed as I am now. I will go tomorrow morning and simply say to Gurdjieff, 'I will do.' Just those three words, but for me, before myself, they will be the authentic beginning of my life. When I say those words I will see before me a succession of unknown experiences which I will pass through, without perceiving the end. My end, I believed, would be my death. Now there comes an end before the end, a death before my death. And it is to win a life.

*October 19.* Five o'clock in the morning, in my room, Casimir Perier. The sky is pale blue behind the still trees. All is happy and calm. Why, why did I have to learn that one can live beyond this easy, lovely human life? I loved that life. . . .

At eleven o'clock Margaret and I will ask Gurdjieff to begin.

. . . *Later.* He has agreed, and given us a rendezvous at his house tomorrow at one.

*October 20, late afternoon.* Divine weather in the Luxembourg Gardens. I sat on a bench near the fountain and thought about the new work Gurdjieff had explained this morning in a manner so clear, so total, that I understood it without understanding all his words. For me it is the long-awaited revelation, so real that it has infinite repercussions in my being.

Many years ago—it may be forty—I wrote to Maeterlinck: 'I do not know if you understand me—I am comparable to a bubble that floats in the air and is attached to nothing real; even in the depths of myself I feel that I *am not.* One single preoccupation, perhaps, exists in this void—it is my anxiety at seeing myself thus; and as if, to change, I must accomplish something unknown. It comes from very far in me, like a lost idea, a commandment to which I can give no form; and I search, I search. . . .'

Today, a life later, now that I have found at last what one can *do,* I see again those words, 'As if, to change, I must accomplish something unknown.'

154

# Cette Autre Chose

*Eleven o'clock at night.* Today, this twentieth of October, 1937, I have lived a few real moments.

*End of December.* I am living too hard, I am tired, my sleep is made of paper.

If at this moment I saw death approaching, I would not accept it as I did in the hospital beds where I spent so many months. Now my time is heavy with a true abundance of which I have never dreamed.

I said to Gurdjieff, 'I am almost afraid—life rises in me like the sea.' He repeated, 'It is only a small beginning.'

*The Lighthouse, summer, 1938*

Now that I have collected my notes written during my 'change of route', I am struck by an essential paradox which I find hard to understand. What was that anguish, that despair, which was in me and yet so far from me? It took place so far from my lived life that it never had a voice, not one audible cry. Why that pain when I had no pain? Is the 'soul', then, really elsewhere? I did not know it had to suffer so to beget itself. Since it is my life, how could it have been so outside my human days?

I write these words in the circle of a flashlight, in order not to disturb the two sleepers who might see a glow in my room and think me ill. I had been sleeping after assembling my notes, this afternoon and all evening. Now it is night—three o'clock in the morning. Through the window the moon and its reflection in the water touch my bed . . . I was asleep and suddenly my sleep was torn in two by an idea: where did that despair of which I wrote take place, when my life was so happy? . . . The circle of light falls clearly on my notebook, I hear the silky pulsation of a passing boat, a red glow moves

# Cette Autre Chose

across the ceiling . . . I have lived for years in the shadow of
a deep preoccupation which, however, clarified me and uncovered many things to my sight. Is it that my subconscious
has its own life which does not identify itself with mine? Mine
could be in peace while the other was living its own personal
drama? That drama is like a love that has no name, no face, and
that struggles perpetually to take a form, to BE and to give
being to someone. That someone was I, who did not know it.

# VIII

## 'EVERYTHING'

WHAT, EXACTLY, was the change that had
taken place in us? It had happened so
slowly that it was imperceptible for a
long time, even to our friends.

Gradually we had begun to ask ourselves what
our former attitudes, standards, ideas and behaviour
had to do with Gurdjieff's transvaluations. And we
had to answer: very little.

As Orage had said, objective thinking means
coming to the end of subjective thinking and then
doing something else. So all our efforts were
directed towards discovering that something else.

In our quest of self-discovery, Jane once suggested that we make 'kaleidoscopes' of our lives,
past and present. We worked hard at them, trying
to keep them free of self-delusion; but it was sometimes depressing to realize how slowly we came
upon more exact self-knowledge.

Georgette offered one of her kaleidoscopes for

comment and criticism, and I still have the letter in which Jane discussed it:

Very good, but in our present state the combinations in the kaleidoscope are limited because every individual starts out as a different combination of chemicals from every other. Every individual has many sets of these combinations; the conditions under which he develops determine which set he shall bring forth. Because there is no conscious chemist in the laboratory, only a few chemicals ever come into action, and they come into action mechanically through the action of environment, and through the inter-action with other chemistries of other beings. Once set in motion these chemicals make patterns which we call characteristics, and repeat and repeat. (Habit.) All of this remains in the biological realm, and in that realm the combinations may be very great, but not unlimited.

On the other hand, if there were a chemist in the laboratory the combinations could be infinite . . . all potentialities. The conscious chemist is, of course, the 'Gurdjieff Method'.

In your kaleidoscope of today there is a long paragraph lamenting the loss of love which is a key paragraph to use in an effort to 'conquer illusion'. You must show that you have learned that instinctive love—in its manifestations of attraction, repulsion, sacrifice, courage, crime, etc., its mechanical and chemical combinations that we call love, courtship, marriage, children, family, etc..—is only the human equivalent of that great laboratory in which Nature is the chemist. Your *interpretation* of those chemical manifestations was your love-image—and an illusion.

'To be in a state of instinctive love is to be in a state of danger, and to be dangerous—to oneself or to the other or to both. Because we are polarized to a great force, it is only fortune that keeps us from damaging someone. Love without knowledge is demoniac.' And to lament, suffer, explain, justify—all of this is to show lack of knowledge, lack of strength.

In another paragraph there is something feverish, as if you had not yet been cured of the illness . . . not aloof, non-identified. It is my opinion that you should destroy the last vestige of that old love-image in your effort to understand it; that you should in the future—(having established the first therapeutic condition: wish to cure yourself)—resolve never again to cast one lingering look in the direction of the past, refuse to allow any associations to drag up any part of it; put the whole experience where it belongs: in another time, belonging to another person. Dismiss Maeterlinck from your mind and memory—consciously. You are allowing a mortgage to stand, against your own development. When you speak of resentment, calumny, hatred shown towards you . . . they are only the negative side of something you thought divine when it was manifesting itself positively. Do not stand back and register horror, surprise, or the inability to understand.

Try to show that your confusion of emotions, or mind, was a lack of knowledge in respect of the two

159

men. You had a great love with Maeterlinck and a great
physical experience with the other. Neither you nor
they had any power, direction, or control over any of
it. They were as powerless in their lacks as in their love.
It is insanity to speak of beings as if they were capable of
acting consciously; and if one *does* act consciously, who
is there to understand such action?

What centre was in love with Maeterlinck?—(rarely
all three centres function in any love, and never at the
same time). How much did you love the image of yourself that he created with his words?—love yourself in
him? ('the woman on a pedestal'). How long were you
invulnerable? ('All true loves are invulnerable to every-
body but their beloved'). Infidelity is a sign that the
physical centre has grown indifferent; the basis of instinctive love has a shift of its centre of gravity; or one
was not, at the moment, mentally or perhaps emotionally in love with the beloved, thus taking one off one's
guard and making one's organism unfaithful. Here is a
grand field for investigating the illusion.

Investigate (in your present state of development) the
reactions in you to love. Did you make an illusion of
those reactions, or have you had the illusion that you
made an illusion? Is it all an hallucination that you loved
Maeterlinck as you think you loved him? Did you love
him at all? Did you love your ideal of love? Are you
sure that it isn't a super-Maeterlinckian fantasy . . . all
this love, this suffering? Has it any reality? Didn't you
start wrong? Weren't the original elements (vaguenesses,
pride of the mind, self-love, vanity, art, the theatre) the

elements that were difficult to break with when the time arrived that love was over? You have said so, or have intimated it. Try to formulate it in terms of the Method.

It is vivifying to re-examine our years in New York during the war when people urged us to talk about Gurdjieff and his ideas, and we made great efforts to do it without proselytizing. It was often difficult to make the right impression.

I remember one night when, after a long and, we thought, clarifying exposition, helplessness overcame me when one of our audience began to pace up and down the living-room of our New York house, expounding her own understanding of what we had been saying.

'It must all come down to this, I think—you do your best to accomplish some good in the world, you try to help others, you are nice to everyone. If there's any expectation of heaven, you've done all you can.'

She was a very 'nice' person, and I wanted to tell her a story. One night when we were dining with Gurdjieff in Paris someone said, 'Such a nice man, Mr. Gurdjieff, who came to lunch today.'

'Yes,' Gurdjieff said, 'nice man—because here at table was asleep. Everyone nice when asleep. But you press on one of his corns and then you see what kind of man he is.'

Everyone always asked, 'Is there a personal God in the Gurdjieff theory?'

When we said, 'There is not', they became angry. We tried to elucidate: Gurdjieff once compared our relationship to 'God' as the relationship between us and the bacteria-population of our bodies. These billions of bacteria can have no knowledge of *us*; just as we can have no knowledge of God. Nevertheless it can be said that the bacteria exist, that we exist, and that 'God' exists.

More anger. . . . Then Jane would say, 'The idea of a personal God is the most egotistical gesture of man. That a divine omnipotent being should be concerned with our transient life! Those who love the personal-God idea are those who serve a thousand personal gods—art, vanity, etc. One of you here shows in five minutes that she believes in a personal god: her own judgment of other people's acts. The Gurdjieff method is a method to rid you of personal gods.'

'No one has ever loved a God as we love ourselves.'

Few people were able to understand Gurdjieff's talk about the 'I'—man's potentiality of development. And everyone was annoyed by his concept of man as a machine. 'If that's true,' one of our antagonists said, 'all *I* can say that a machine is a wonderful thing.'

'Yes,' Jane said, 'but it's not a wonderful thing for a man to be.'

Some of our most violent discussions were about Gurdjieff's idea of 'Chief Feature'.

'Every man has a chief feature. It is an outgrowth of his emotional attitude towards himself. Our life is controlled by these chief features. They are founded on vanity (self-love), fear, greed, sex, and lying.'

'Why is he so drastic?' people asked. 'He gives no hope for anyone.'

We always felt that he held out the only hope. Not that we were over-confident about our own self-development, but it surprised us that many people didn't respond to his ideas as we did. Sometimes we gave up.

We had an English friend who often came to ask questions and to air her own views. At first I thought her questions rather searching, and I began to hope that she would finally understand what Gurdjieff had in mind.

Then one night, after she had been silent for a long time, she addressed Jane in a social voice. 'Tell me, Jane—is Gurdjieff a . . . gentleman?'

Incredible as it now seems to me, I've forgotten

Jane's answer. Perhaps she only laughed. But I remember how she answered Rom Landau, who wanted to put Gurdjieff's idea of the octave into a book he was writing, *God is My Adventure*, and asked Jane to help him. 'Formulate what you want to say,' she wrote to him, 'and if there's anything I can do I'll do it.' After his formulation Jane wrote: 'All your problems are solved—(octave, nature, scope, function)—and explained in Gurdjieff's chapter "Purgatory" and amplified in chapter "Eptaparaparshinock". Your formulation does not contact the world of thinking in which the Gurdjieff octave has a place.'

To avoid philosophizing, our talks sometimes went like this:

One night, in an argument, a scoffer challenged me by saying, 'Now tell me, if you can, who is the Holy Ghost?'

'I can try,' I said, 'if you'll ask me *what* instead of *who*.'

'Oh, I'll ask, but I'm sure you can't answer.'

'Well,' I said, 'you know about positive and negative electric currents?'

'Certainly.'

'What makes them produce light—in this lamp, for instance?'

'They pass through a transformer in some electric power plant?'

'All right. You can call that transformer a third force. So you have three forces—positive, negative, and neutralizing. Always three. Every "event", every situation, every actualization, every phenomenon, is a result of three forces acting together. The third force—(the neutralizing or form-giving force)—which brings the other two together can be called the Holy Ghost.'

'Why? Who says so?'

'Why don't *you* say? Can't you think of a simple answer?—an illustration?'

'No. All I can think of is "In the name of the Father, the Son, and the Holy Ghost".'

'All right,' I said, 'take a father. He's an active, positive force. Take a mother—she's a passive, negative force. They produce a child. But there's no child unless positive force meets negative force. What is the third force that brings them together?'

'They must feel an attraction.'

'All right . . . then your answer is Desire. In this case, desire is the Holy Ghost.'

'Well, well,' she said—'perfectly simple, n'est ce pas?'

'Perhaps,' I said. 'But then you must stretch the idea out to take in the creation of the universe.'

'Oh,' she said. Then, 'But that I can't do. Can you?'

'No,' I said. 'But we can think about it.'

Almost everyone was shocked by Gurdjieff's statement that 'the whole foundation of man's essence has become the psychic properties of cunning, envy, hate, hypocrisy, contempt, slyness, ambition, double-facedness'.

'Why doesn't he include love? Many people are motivated by love.'

'Yes?' Jane would answer. 'Let's have a little precision.' And she would formulate in her own words some of the ideas about love in Gurdjieff's *All and Everything*:

*Love is always of three kinds:* Instinctive (or physical) love. Emotional love. Conscious love.

*Physical love* depends on type and polarity—a person whose type influences your chemistry.

*Emotional love* begets the opposite emotion—hate.

*Conscious love* begets love of a like kind.

The statement about emotional love usually provoked fierce debates. 'It's the most ideal type of love,' someone always insisted.

Jane would continue:

*Emotional love* is pathologic. The lover is a medium through which an uncontrolled power of magnetism passes. Emotional lovers are the victims of their own unconscious power. Emotional love always creates hate in the lover, then in the loved one, then back again—an eternal changing of the hate. Emotional love seldom produces offsprings. It is non-biological. It evokes its own slayer.

## 'Everything'

*Physical love* has chemistry as its basis. And it lasts as long as, and is only as strong as, that chemistry. This is the highest type of love we know, because of its radiations—(since we know little about conscious love).

*Conscious love* wishes that the loved object should arrive at its own native perfections, regardless of the consequences to the lover. The paradox: it always evokes the same love in the beloved. This type is rare among us.

'Christ was love!' someone would always announce at this point.

Jane: 'Christ appealed to love. It didn't exist strongly enough. It exists less strongly now. He appealed to something that wasn't there.'

And she went on: 'In these talks, you must always know which realm you are talking in—(1) the *status-quo* world (the world at any given moment, as we now are; or (2) the *dynamic* world—the world of *becoming*. Distinguish always between these two worlds. And when you talk of Christ, try to think of the crucifixion as a *conscious* act in a *conscious* drama.'

In the 1920's and 30's, when Orage was lecturing in New York, he used a terminology that I found specially rewarding. For example:

'A body is an organization. The physical body is an organization; just so, the emotional body is an organization; the mental body also. What is the energy we use to create a higher emotional and mental body? We must use an energy that is stronger than the mind or the emotions. When Nature created us she created a surplus energy—that which goes into ideals, etc. This surplus was created for higher consciousness. Its conscious use is self-development, self-perfectionment.'

And this:

'Emotions and ideas have the same persistence as physical objects (the persistence is relative). Discrimination of emotions and ideas as if they were objects is the development of astral formal reason. But until your organism is as objective for you as any object, you cannot have any sense of the quality of objective reason.'

'The ability to discriminate between words and their associations = verbal reason. The ability to discriminate between emotions and ideas = formal reason. Verbal discrimination—that is, speculative reason—is rated lowest by Gurdjieff because it does not lead to formal or objective reason. (This is why he says "Don't philosophize".)

'I wish to arouse an abandonment of the attempt to formulate objective reason. There is nothing in objective reason that is a shadow of subjective reason. Objective reason means coming to the end of subjective reason and then having an experience that is totally different.'

*Pupil:* 'Is it possible to attain formal reason?'

*Orage:* 'Voluntary suffering is an effort to have personal experience in place of what has been verbal or associative

168

experience. Objective reason implies the ability to think without being affected by conditioning or heredity. It is different from the reasoning we know. (This is why, Margaret, you are baffled by Gurdjieff at the table.)

'The Gurdjieff science is a *science of experience*. The question to be asked is: "Is the report a part of transient knowledge or of permanent knowledge?" You can find this only for yourself, by working on yourself. What is a real experience? One in which the whole being takes part—a whole experience. You know it when it happens. Experience to be anything must belong to a system of things—the affirmed emotions of mankind.'

In New York, in 1946, when we were planning our return to Paris and Gurdjieff, I remember one night when we tried to keep the discussion strictly within the frame of the Gurdjieff cosmology. We had got as far as man's potentiality, of which he knows nothing; from there to the possible development of his three centres, so that they could act together instead of separately; then to the definition of the octave and man's function—his transference from one scale to another.

Solita quoted some words of Gurdjieff's: 'One must *strive* for Being. If anyone desires to know and understand more than he knows and understands, he must remember that this new knowledge and new understanding will come through the emotional centre and not through the mental centre.'

'But', she added, 'he also said "Study; study everything. Know yourself, then humanity, then the planet. Study forty-eight hours a day".'

Someone asked, 'But after you've studied and worked and understood, then what do you do? Or isn't there anything else to the Gurdjieff theory?'

Everyone was silent, everyone looked at everyone else. I looked at Solita. What could she say? I could only think of things too long to say.

Dorothy too looked at her. 'Is there anything beyond all this, Solita?'

'Yes.'

'What comes afterwards?' Dorothy asked.

'Everything,' said Solita.

## IX

## APARTMENT IN PARIS

IN JUNE, 1948, all of us who had been stranded in America during the war returned to France —and to Gurdjieff.

Paris was not the same . . . it was lovelier. There were fewer people in the streets—'this air, this stone, this earth, this water' . . . all were more visible and conspired to break the heart.

Gurdjieff's small dingy familiar apartment in the rue des Colonels Renard had not changed—details of destruction only emphasized its changelessness: the colours had faded, the furniture was shabbier, the dining-room carpet had worn through and now had big patches on it. Nine years and a war had brought new people to the remembered table, but their quest was the old quest, the same as ours. The pictures on the walls were new, but they had the same quality as the old ones—'everything but art', as Jane had said long ago. All was as it had been,

171

including the presence, as always, of a stranger who was seeing Gurdjieff for the first time. And we were all there again together—except Georgette.* The newest newcomer was Dorothy Caruso.

Gurdjieff himself seemed to me unchanged. He was a little older, he was a little tired, but he was still as lavish as ever with his existence and his ceremony. He sat at the side of the table, instead of at the end, and he was more silent than in the years before. But there was teaching in all that he did or said, only its form had changed: he was teaching now chiefly through his presence—from his 'being', he might have said. A stranger might have thought he was unconscious of what was taking place around him; but we were alert to his awareness of everyone's words and gestures, to his monosyllabic indications of type and tendency. We listened with all our force to his rapid or elaborated, terse or kindly, criticism of human egoism; he let no slight failing pass without signal or correction. Most of the old pupils felt that he was gentler than in the old years. I could only feel that his weariness with the human condition had reached the breaking-point. But we knew that he would fulfil to the end his obligation to life.

There were now so many new pupils—English and American and French—that he transmitted

* Georgette Leblanc died in 1941.

much of his instruction through a person we had
known in the old Prieuré days. After years of work
with him her stature was now visible to everyone.
Her name was Jeanne de Salzmann.

We lunched with him every day, and usually
returned for dinner at nine. Before every meal one
of the older pupils read from *Beelzebub's Tales to
His Grandson*.

Late one afternoon in July Dorothy and I were
having tea in the park between the American Em-
bassy and the Champs Elysées. A group of chatter-
ing people sat at the table next to ours, and nothing
could have been more startling than to hear, in
such a place, in such a group, the name of Gurdjieff.
A 'best-dressed' man was repeating the usual de-
tractions, calumnies, that one is accustomed to hear
when the unknowing talk of Gurdjieff.

'Don't say anything,' Dorothy begged. 'It's useless. Let's just go.'

As we left I lingered behind her and stopped
before the group, and spoke in a slow quiet voice.
'May I say, in passing, that none of the things
you've been saying about Gurdjieff is true?'

There was a loud silence, then a burst of unsure
laughter from one of the women. I walked on, and
all the way up the Champs Elysées I breathed deep
breaths of pleasure and triumph.

Some time later I was told that one of the group

had gone to Madame de Salzmann to ask what Gurdjieff was really like.

During 1948 and 1949 we saw Gurdjieff almost continuously, and Dorothy has written of her experience in her book *Dorothy Caruso: A Personal History* (Hermitage House). Her story, too, differs from all others. It is told simply, without the slightest intellectual pretention.

It began with our meeting on the S.S. *Drottlingholm*, in 1942, when we were returning to New York after having lived through almost two years of war in France:

*June*, 1942

. . . I was returning after an absence of ten transilient years to New York—a gigantic city filled with strangers and forgotten friends, that once had been my home and was my home no longer.

I faced a future without plan or purpose. After my rapturous past and my astonishing present, all that I had to look forward to was a life of ease and emptiness.

Three tenses, defined and flat and narrow as ribbons— could that be all there was to life—to everyone's life? There must be another tense, a fourth, without a name. . . . When I tried to follow my thought to its conclusion it wavered away, dimmed and disappeared, like a star that is lost when you look at it directly.

I remembered the night in Paris years ago, when

something had come close—the shadow of a mystery.... Now I perceived a faint form behind the shadow. Then all at once the whole thought vanished. There was no fourth tense, or star, or mystery. No wonderful experience was waiting for me anywhere.

A return to reason in a dreaded world would be my only experience.

## A CONVERSATION

I was wrong.

Two nights later on the ship, twenty-four hours out of New York, I sat unconscious of time and sea, conscious only of a conversation.

In darkness, on a deserted deck, I looked up into the black unmoving sky and listened to words that lighted the universe.

They were words that contained thoughts of such power and abstraction, such virtue and vastness, that I sat speechless, overwhelmed by the magnitude of ideas of a kind I had never heard.

All my own thoughts, all my uneasy unsuccessful efforts to create within my troubled mind a mental chart that I could follow towards what I hoped would be a wonderful experience, became puerile, pitiful, in the face of an immense unknown world that was opening before me. It reached far beyond the mind and yet was a part of it, or the mind a part of its immensity.

In my flash of understanding, the words I was hearing were consumed, forgotten for ever, and I saw instead a way of life, a road as clear, as straight, as the road I saw

175

in that instant when I looked at Enrico Caruso from the top of a flight of stairs.

At two o'clock I went to my cabin. The children were waiting for me. 'Something has happened to me,' I said. 'I have heard things tonight that may change the course of our lives.'

The person who made this conversation was Margaret Anderson.

But I could not repeat the words I had heard—even today I cannot remember a single phrase of that conversation. It had to do with a system of knowledge concerning man's relation to God and the universe, as taught by a man called Gurdjieff. He lived in Paris and for many years had been teaching there. From a name, and an outline of an 'unknown doctrine', there arose for me a total vision of a new world. What was important, now, was how soon I and my children could enter this world.

And suddenly I realized, as if through revelation, that on this night, on a ship sailing towards New York, I had come at last within sight of a land I had sought since childhood.

The magnitude of the revelation, the quality of the disclosure and the immensity of its effect upon me, erased from my mind all dread of the future. Nothing could ever take from me this night's apperception of a new world; and my only wish was to meet the man called Gurdjieff who had explored to its limits this unknown world, who had travelled all the way along its roads and welcomed all those in need who came to him to learn.

*Chez Gurdjieff, Paris*
*June,* 1948

In spite of all I had been told, I had made my own conception of Gurdjieff. He would have the tongue of St. John, the inspiration of St. Paul, the sanctity and remoteness of the Reverend Mother. I would be filled with awe and exaltation, and when I left it would be with a high sense of humility for the privilege of having met him.

It was in this fervent and expectant state that I entered his Paris flat in the rue Colonel Renard on the last day of June.

But when I saw Gurdjieff all my preconceived ideas vanished. For I saw an old man, grey with weariness and illness, yet whose strength of spirit emanated with such force from his weakened body that, save for a sense of fierce protection, I felt no deep emotion at all.

I could not understand his English. His low voice and muffled Asiatic accent formed syllables that had no meaning to me, and at the same time I realized that at this moment ordinary speech was unimportant. It was as if we had already spoken and were continuing to speak, but in a language without sound.

There were twenty pupils lunching with him that first day. Except for an occasional low murmur they sat in silence, watchful, unsmiling. When Gurdjieff spoke they sat up straighter, tensed as if their backbones had suddenly solidified.

## Apartment in Paris

He sat relaxed, with one foot folded under him, on a divan opposite us, slowly eating morsels of lamb and hard bits of goat cheese and fresh tarragon leaves with his fingers. His eyebrows rose above his lowered lids when a murmur reached him, but he did not turn his head to look—he seemed to see without looking.

At the end of the meal he began to talk. I scarcely understood a word, but I was galvanized to a zenith of attention: every expression of his face and each small movement of his body I found heartbreaking. I thought, 'The kind of force he is using is wearing him out. Why must he go on doing it? Why do they let him? We should go home, we should not ask this tired man for anything.'

But as we left he said, 'You come tonight for reading at nine o'clock. Then dinner after.' I thanked him, told him I thought he was too tired. I might have been speaking with one of my children instead of to a man of eighty-one—a magus, a possessor of super-knowledge.

I sat in the corner of the salon before dinner, listening to a chapter from his manuscript read aloud . . . an expressionless voice going on and on, pupils seated on the floor, motionless and intense.

The next night I listened again, and the night after. Day after day and night after night I listened to that unimpassioned voice and watched those immobile faces —some with open unseeing eyes, some with eyes closed. There was no continuity in the reading—chapters read the week before were repeated the following week, or

sometimes a chapter read half through was never re-
sumed. After a while my attention wandered, but that
of the pupils on the floor did not. The concentration of
those motionless bodies began to irritate me.

What were they concentrated on? Surely not on the
manuscript which they must have heard a hundred
times. Perhaps they were reflecting on the great ideas of
Gurdjieff; but I couldn't detect ideas in the allegory of
*Beezelbub's Tales to His Grandson* that was being read
aloud.

A month passed. I had learned to understand Gurdjieff's broken English but I had not once heard him
present a great idea. I was told that he was no longer
teaching through ideas, as he had done at the Prieuré
twenty-five years before. But I could in no way relate
the man I saw every day to the mystic Gurdjieff I had
heard about from Margaret, on a boat, six years ago. Of
course he talked, but chiefly of countries and national-
ities, and always in a large derogatory way, as repetitious
and boring as the readings. Or else he scolded the pupils
who prepared the food. He spoke harshly and, I thought,
unjustly; I felt it was humiliating to be reprimanded
before everyone. Usually the pupil remained quiet but
when, during the tirade, he dared to defend himself,
Gurdjieff's voice grew louder, angrier, and his eyes
flashed. Then at the peak of rage he suddenly smiled,
relaxed, and said 'Bravo!' and offered the culprit his
favourite sweet. Why? What had all this to do with the
universe and man and his immortality?

And if those pupils seated on the floor during the interminable readings were not pretending, what then were they thinking, with their lost rapt faces?

I had brought my body into a world of thought. I was an alien in an incomprehensible world. Self-conscious and bewildered, I sat in my corner, listening, trying to understand.

At last a day came when I told Margaret that I had had enough: it was useless for me to go on seeing Gurdjieff.

'I might as well fly back to America. I'm not learning anything. He isn't teaching anything. What is there to learn, just listening to that book, watching the others who never speak to me, whose names I don't even know, and watching Gurdjieff eat or play that little organ? I'm going home.'

'You must do as you think best,' Margaret said. She neither urged me to stay nor seemed concerned about my going. For five days I stayed away. Then I went back to Gurdjieff.

I went back because he had been so kind to me. He hadn't railed at me, or frightened me. Indeed, at our third meeting he had said—apropos of nothing, it seemed to me—'Inside you are rabbit.' I had wondered at the time how he knew. I still wondered.

Another reason for going back was a conventional one: I had dined with him every night for a month; it was boorish to leave without saying good-bye or thanking him. Besides, I had missed him more each day I stayed away. After all, if he wasn't teaching in the way

I had expected, perhaps he was teaching in another way.

He did not reproach me for my absence. He simply smiled, and pretended to be surprised to see me. And at the crowded table he even teased me a little about my size. It was a warm and vibrant welcome, and during lunch I felt a glow as if there had been established between us a new and special bond—a kind of unspoken sympathetic understanding.

After lunch he invited me to have coffee with him in his store-room. There, in the midst of fruits and sweets and wines, with slender sausages of camel's meat, bunches of scarlet peppers and sprays of rosemary and mint suspended like a canopy above, as I watched him pouring coffee out of the battered old thermos bottle, I suddenly felt as young and trustful as I had felt when Mother Thompson watched over me in the Convent. Years of worldly experience fell away and I was a child again.

Gurdjieff offered me a piece of sugar. 'You want to ask me something?' he said. I didn't want to ask him anything—I wanted to tell him something. But I was unprepared for this direct and simple opening. I could not quickly think of any abstract or esoteric question, so instead I blurted out what had troubled me ever since I had been going to his house.

'Everyone here seems to have a soul except me. Haven't I any soul?'

He didn't answer immediately, or look at me. He took a piece of sugar, put it into his mouth and sipped some coffee through it. Then he said, 'You know what means consciousness?'

'Yes,' I said, 'it means to know something.'

'No. Not to know something—to know yourself. Your "I". You not know your "I" for one second in your whole life. Now I tell and you try. But very difficult. You try remember say "I am" once every hour. You not succeed, but no matter—try. You understand?'

At this first interview I said none of the things I had planned to say. Instead I told him about my childhood in my father's house, of the goodness of Enrico and my despair when he died, and about my children and how deeply I loved them. And then I said, 'I don't know anything about the things all the others know. I don't even know what to ask you. What can I do when I have nothing to start from? What shall I *do*?'

'You must help your father,' Gurdjieff said. I thought he had not understood, that I had spoken too quickly; so I told him again that my father was dead.

'I know. You tell already. But because of your father you are here. Have gratitude for this. You are your father and you owe to him. He is dead. Too late to repair for himself. You must repair for him. Help him.'

'But how can I help him when he's dead? Where is he?'

'All around you. You must work on yourself. Remember what I tell—your "I". And what you do for yourself you do also for me.'

He said no more but I felt as if he had spoken great

things, and not in ordinary words; and when I left it was
with something rich and strange and full of meaning.

No matter how late, each night in the salon after
dinner Gurdjieff took his little accordion-piano on his
knee and, while his left hand worked the bellows, his
right hand made music in minor chords and haunting
single notes.

But one night in his aromatic store-room he played
for five of us, alone, a different kind of music, although
whether the difference lay in its sorrowful harmonies or
in the way he played I do not know. I only know that
no music had ever been so sad. Before it ended I put my
head on the table and wept.

'What has happened to me?' I said. 'When I came
into this room I was happy. And then that music—and
now I am happy again.'

'I play objective music to make cry,' Gurdjieff said.
'There are many kinds such music—some to make laugh,
or to love or to hate. This the beginning of music—
sacred music, two, three thousand years old. Your
church music comes from such but they don't realize.
They have forgotten. This is temple music—very ancient.'

Once when he played I thought the music sounded
like a prayer—it seemed to supplicate. And then I
thought, 'It is only my imagination and my emotion,'
and I tried not to feel what I was feeling. But when he
had finished, instead of smiling and tapping the top of
the instrument with his hand, he sat quite still and his

eyes stood motionless, as if he were looking at us through his thoughts. Then he said, 'It is a prayer,' and left us.

*Midsummer.* Gurdjieff was leaving by car, with some of his pupils, to take the baths at Vichy. I was happy to be free for a while, away from the heat of his flat and the smell of heavy soup cooking. I longed to breathe fresh air again, to see fields and animals instead of people. I was tired of people and their inner lives, and I was most tired of thinking about my own. I would go to Normandy with Margaret, to a small hotel in the village of Giverny. There we would walk along country roads in sunshine, look through a gate into Claude Monet's garden—scarlet poppies, marigolds, delphiniums, daisies, under arches of bright roses. We would sit beside his pool, where pale and pointed water-lilies lay and long willow branches touched the water. We would work again on our books—we hadn't thought of books since we left Sudbury.

In my room at the Hotel Baudy my work-table faced a window. I saw peasants mowing hay on a quiet hillside. The smell of new-mown hay and the chirp of sun-drenched birds came in at the open window.

I began once more to write . . .

. . . Three days passed and a message came from Paris late at night. Gurdjieff had been injured in a motor accident. His condition was critical; he was lying unconscious in a hospital.

When we arrived in Paris he was already at home. He

had fractured ribs, lacerations on his face and hands, and many bruises. There was a danger of internal injuries.

'Is he conscious now?'

'Oh yes,' they said, 'and he wants the readings and meals to continue as usual. He came in for a little while after lunch. He'll be at dinner—thirty are coming.'

But the next day he was worse and the doctors held out slight hope that he would live.

We stayed that night in a small hotel near his flat, waiting for the telephone to ring. It never rang. On the third day he was seated again at his dinner table. His head was still a shining dome, smooth and high, but his face was a dark shadow. There were purple bruises on his lips and he wore a piece of gauze around his throat to hide a wound.

'I cannot eat,' he said, 'my mouth all cut inside.' Painfully, with his lacerated fingers, he divided a trout, handed me a piece across the table.

'You like?' he said. 'Then take.'

For the rest of the meal he sat in silence. In his eyes was the same blind look he had when he played the prayer music. As we rose to leave he got up too. He lifted his hands against his ribs. 'It hurts,' he said, 'great suffering I have.' I could only stand there looking at him. Before I could wish him well, he said, 'I thank you. I wish for you all that you wish for me.'

He cured himself, no one knew how. He had refused X-rays and the medicines prescribed by doctors; yet his recovery was so complete that he looked younger after the accident than before, as if the shock had strengthened his whole organism instead of weakening it.

In the late afternoon he sat, immaculately dressed, outside a café near his flat, with a panama hat shading his eyes and his cane lying across the table in front of him, talking with pupils, drinking coffee, watching people pass. At other times he sat alone, speaking with no one, noticing no one until at last he rose and, in the long dusk, through quiet shuttered streets, walked slowly home.

There, after resting for a while, he changed into a loose grey cashmere suit, open white shirt and soft kid slippers, gave instructions in the kitchen, then came to sit with us and listen to the reading of his book, looking from one face to another, recognizing yet withholding recognition. At dinner he welcomed us as he had always done, talked of the same subjects in the same words; and, as usual, half-way through the meal, placed on his head his tasselled magenta fez. It was good to know that he was recovering, and it was good to see and hear intimate small ceremonies repeated—the ritual of the toasts, the offering of bread, or fish, across the table in his hand. And as I sat observing, absorbing, rejoicing, I grew aware of a swelling sense of harmony that related everything within the room to everything else—gestures, faces, voices, food, my thoughts vibrated in unison like a chord in music. I began to understand something that I longed to go on understanding. I wanted to achieve the 'I' he had told me about.

Long before his accident Gurdjieff had said, 'I cannot

develop you; I can create the conditions in which you can develop yourself.' For weeks I had fought against the conditions he created—I had been angry, impatient, judicial. But I had concealed these emotions; raging inside, I had appeared outwardly calm . . . the habit of a lifetime—good manners, instead of an effort to act honestly. It would have been better to burst forth in defence of what I thought unjust, to ask him point-blank why I should sit through endless meals, eating food I neither liked nor wanted. That I had felt compassion or anxiety or even deep affection for him was beside the point. It was good to be concerned about him; it would have been better to have been concerned about myself: to have begun to change, to develop myself. Once he had spoken to me about my great aim. 'I haven't any aim,' I said; 'what should my aim be?' He said, 'Do you want to perish like a dog?' I answered, 'Of course not.' He didn't explain, he simply repeated what he had said before: 'Remember your "I".'

*Christmas*, 1948. Back in America, I told my children all that had happened to me in Paris. Gloria listened, holding her new son, Colin, in her arms. Before his birth Gurdjieff had said, 'Good that mother should worry for her child—he will be strong.' And Jackie listened, with three-year-old Dolly sitting beside her. I had asked Gurdjieff Jackie's question: 'How shall I introduce God to my baby?' His answer was, 'All babies near God. Later, bring to me and I will tell.'

Gurdjieff had arrived in New York in time for Christmas. Instead of fifty pupils, as in Paris, he now sometimes had a hundred in his hotel-apartment—often as many as eighty for dinner. He worked with them constantly, never resting, never sparing himself. At the same time he was arranging for the publication of his book, *All and Everything*. Each night it was read aloud; each night until two in the morning he played his music for us. After we left he slept for three hours, then rose and drove down to the big bright markets at the end of the city, to choose fresh food for the feasts of the coming day. He stayed in New York for two months, and when he went back to France we followed him.

It was May in Paris, but for us there was no spring. There was no time to notice horse-chestnut trees blossoming in the Bois, or illuminated fountains sparkling in the Place de la Concorde in the soft sweet night. There was time only to drive as fast as possible by the shortest route to Gurdjieff's flat in the rue Colonel Renard—a street with as little French distinction as a page in a dictionary; a flat without sunlight or a single flower, where the motionless air reeked of Asiatic cooking and the heat was almost unbearable.

The contrast between Gurdjieff's strong decisive bearing and the deep hollows in his face alarmed me. 'I am very tired,' he said, 'I work too hard.' 'You should take a vacation,' I said. 'I have no time—many people come from England to see me in these days. There is still much to do.' Later he said, 'I would like to go to Chamonix—to hear water running; there I could sleep.'

Another month of pupils, meals and heat. Then one night he said, 'We go to Chamonix tomorrow.' He asked us to go along.

Four motor-cars were crowded with pupils, with boxes of Russian croquettes, bags of *croissants*, melons, apricots, chocolate bon-bons and big thermos bottles of black coffee. Gurdjieff drove his car all the way, leading the caravan. He used no maps, gave no directions; he simply said, 'Follow me,' and started off, stopping only to nap for a half hour by the side of the road when he could go no farther.

In Chamonix he wakened in the mornings refreshed by the splashing icy stream beneath his window. But his days were as active as in Paris—devoted to his work, his business affairs and the responsibility of new young pupils. At the week's end, in spite of the cold thin air, the healing pines and fresh snow-winds from the mountains, he was still tired.

I sat beside him on a bench outside the hotel the day we left Chamonix, watching the porters arrange luggage in the cars. At last I said, 'May I tell you something, Mr. Gurdjieff? I wish I had met you twenty years ago. Today it's too late. I realize now that I am nothing, and it's the loneliest feeling in the world.'

He turned and looked at me: 'Ah,' he said, 'you are no longer blind. Your eyes now open—you begin to see.'

He took some bon-bons from his pocket, handed them to a porter passing by. I had often seen him do this, and always wondered why. 'Why do you offer candy to people?' I asked, 'and why does everyone look pleased—

policemen, waiters, strangers, and that young mother last night sitting in the salon with her baby—why?'

'I do not know if I will see again that mother, but if I do she will not forget me—she will remember the surprise of bon-bons for her baby. Perhaps she will need help and I not be a stranger. You understand?'

'Yes, I understand about the mother, but the policeman . . .?'

'The policeman stopped me. I did not wish to wait—I gave bon-bons and he was very surprised. So he let me go. That is being clever man.'

He was also an ill man—coughing, in pain. Yet back in Paris at his table he still had room for all who came—pupils from England, Scotland, Switzerland, Austria, as well as America.

To spare him we went less, but he noticed our absence and bade us come as usual. He had grown thinner and the grey pallor had returned. One day at lunch he said, 'I have worked hard. My book will soon be published for everyone to read. After I will go away, far, where I can rest.' 'But you will come back?' someone asked. He did not answer. Another said, 'We will follow you wherever you go—will you go to California?' It was the kind of question Gurdjieff never answered, but this time he looked at the speaker and smiled. 'Perhaps California, perhaps farther,' he said.

It was the middle of October—a gold crimson country day when chipmunks rush to gather nuts, and horses, free in pale gold fields, race with each other and the

wind. I left Giverny to see Gurdjieff in his café in Paris—
to say farewell until we should meet on the boat that was
to take us all to America on the twentieth.

He was sitting alone. 'You take coffee?' he said. For a
moment I didn't speak, then when the coffee came I
said, 'You are not coming on the boat with us after all.'
'No. Perhaps later.'

We sat in silence. Finally I said, 'Mr. Gurdjieff . . . the
"I" which I am trying to develop—is this the soul that
survives after death?'

He waited so long that I wondered whether he had
heard me. Then he said, 'How long you have been with
me?'

'Almost two years,' I said.

'Too short the time. You not able yet to understand.
Use the present to repair the past and prepare the future.
Go on well; remember all I say.'

I did not press him—he looked so ill. 'You should
take better care of yourself,' I said; 'what are you doing
for your cough? Does something hurt you?' He moved
slightly in his chair and for the first time I heard from
him a sound like a groan. 'I must take habit of pain,' he
said. Then he held out his hand and I said good-bye, and
left him sitting there, alone, in the shrill sunlight.


## SEA-CHANGE

I never saw Gurdjieff again. He died in Paris, two days
after we landed in New York. And so, scarcely before it
had begun, a great experience ended.

Whatever I may have learned about his work, during the two years I knew him, might, as time passed, grow hazy in my mind; but what I felt when I was in his presence, whether he spoke or sat in silence, I would remember clearly always. Those feelings live for ever that are born in the soul's heart.

Gurdjieff was gentle with my soul. It was a soul that had not grown up, as I grew up. It had been timid, but trusting. Often it had been betrayed, but it had not been murdered. Nanna had found it first, and she too had been gentle with it. Enrico had loved, moulded, sustained and protected it.

Gurdjieff gave it courage. From his mysterious and conscious world he guided it with the kind of understanding he called 'objective love'—the 'love of everything that breathes'; and 'it' responded with unlimited trust—the highest type of love there is, I think, in this immediate and unconscious world.

Nothing is so great or so true as the trusting love of a child. It doesn't matter whether he has understood your words or not—it is the way they are spoken that matters. And the way they are spoken creates in the child the love and trust he returns to you. This is the emotion that Gurdjieff, and the 'conditions he created', created in me.

I can repeat our conversations, interpret his silences, describe his appearance, define his doctrine, yet I can only give the slightest indication of the change that took place in me after knowing him.

I was aware, before he died, of this process of active

and increasing change. His death, instead of ending the process, accelerated it. And then, one day, I understood what had been happening. I had transformed something in myself: the change was Me.


A mystery is something that cannot be expressed, something beyond human comprehension.

Man is a mystery.

The cosmos is a mystery.

Man in relation to the cosmos is a mystery.

Everything is a mystery, and everything is a paradox. To understand this takes more than human comprehension, and more than human comprehension means: to know.

Gurdjieff knew.

He knew from his 'being', as he called it. And he knew all the time.

I know only for an instant at a time. That instant is a spark of understanding—it belongs to the person of my essence. During those instants I am aware of a division of identity—a separation between my essence-person and what I have always called 'myself'.

When those moments are past they do not become simply memories like other memories. Something else raises and widens and deepens the perceptions.

The substance of that 'something' I do not know—all I know is that it is a substance; it is not merely an idea.

Thus far have I gone. What is to come next is, for the present, another mystery.

## Apartment in Paris

All my time is not spent in pondering these things, nor are my thoughts always on eternity or death. But I am actively aware of everything today, instead of passively aware as in the past. I can see each feather on a bird that flies by—it doesn't just fly by.

I have been told that I am simply using my five senses. I am, as always; but the knowledge that I am doing it belongs to that second self. Therefore I can live in splendour in a little house beside a walnut tree in Maryland where everything I touch, or hear, or see, has its reverberations in that world where no one lives except those who have also been as fortunate as I.

Early this morning I went out into the flowering woods behind our house, to think out an ending for this book. I was alone . . . no one passed. The fragrance of uncurling violets, the nursery pink-and-white of dogwood blossoms, my rustling footsteps in the leaves . . . all this young spring I felt, and more than fifty other springs besides, with gratitude to everyone I have known, and an aspiration to love everything that breathes.

*Riderwood, Maryland.*
*April,* 1951

# X

# EVERY MAN IS AN ISLAND

URING OUR last years with Gurdjieff I was
astounded to discover that all my old problems and rebellions had again become ram-
pant. I was so haunted by my self-dissatisfactions,
my self-accusations, that I feared I might never
uncover their cause, or, even if I did, never discover
their cure. My nights were troubled by these fears,
and I often wakened after a long dream of having
fled the hounds of heaven through all the hours of
sleep.

The definite words that haunted me were these:
'Happy is he who has a soul, happy is he who has
not. But grief and sorrow to him who has the
conception and does not accomplish it.'

As usual, when one is full of self-recrimination,
it is all-too-human to concentrate on the short-
comings of others. I must have been insufferable as
I preached to my friends what I should have been
accusing in myself.

'We talk,' I said, 'but nothing happens. None of
you wants to move quickly—"We would like to
benefit by Gurdjieff", you say, "if we can have him
in small doses, when we want it". With such an
attitude there's nothing to do but let *the thing* go
by. It isn't a thing to be taken as one likes, one has
to stretch towards it with all one's strength or not
get it; you can count yourself fortunate if you can
get some of it as it goes by. *It* doesn't wait; *you*
have to do the waiting and the watching and the
effort or you'll be left behind. Your centre of gravity has to be switched from "life" to this "other
thing". If you have a negative attitude you let it
drift by, hoping that some day . . . I'm not at home
in the negative attitude, I come out of it crushed,
obsessed by the conviction that I'm a part of something else, that I must try to stop adjusting to the
*status quo*. You have to make ten times your normal
effort, and even then you can only get as much as
your cell-intelligence permits. You have to be always on tip-toe, ready to sprint ahead.'

Fortunately, having finally learned enough about
the mote-and-the-beam situation to realize that
what I was preaching to others I was not practising
myself, I decided that I must talk with Madame de
Salzmann and ask her to help me. I had always
found her approachable, and I felt that she under-

stood above anyone else certain things in a certain realm—that realm where, if you had progressed sufficiently with Gurdjieff, he could communicate with you almost without words.

'I have always found it difficult to talk with Gurdjieff,' I told her. 'I have so much awe of him that such an informality seems to me to touch upon irreverence.'

'I know,' she said. 'But perhaps you can find someone in the group you can trust, and talk with him as you aren't able to talk with Mr. Gurdjieff.'

'I trust *you*,' I told her, 'and I'm determined not to regard you with such awed admiration that I can't speak. I trust you even to understand my rebellions.'

She laughed, and quoted the beginning lines of *My Thirty Years' War*—'Reality is your greatest enemy?' Then she asked, 'What do you want to say?'

'May I explode?' I said. 'Just this once. I may never need to again.'

'Of course,' she said.

So I began. 'My suffering can be reduced to one essential rebellion,' I said. 'I *cannot* give up all my time to Gurdjieff's work; it makes all other work impossible. I want to write, I think I have special and interesting things to say. But there's no use trying to say them if I haven't the time to put them

into *form*—the only device that will give them
value. In other words, art.'

She said nothing, but sat quietly waiting.

I summoned all my force and tried to put my
problem into clear words: my necessity to be in a
'state' before I could produce anything creative;
and the torture of interrupting such states because
your conscience tells you that you should be doing
something more important.

'How often', I said, 'I remember Gurdjieff's
statement that everyone's personal data is as different from every other person's as his finger-prints,
and that no one understands the subjective states of
another. As I see it, every man is an island. My
island is that place where I am free to live, without
interruption, in my "states". I can never write de-
cently unless I am allowed this concentrated condition. I can never talk well unless I can first enter
into a kind of trance—oh, not what psychics call
trance, you understand, just a special state—and
prolong it until the creative mood arrives. A period
of concentrated life must be given to a book or
there will *be* no book. It's like playing the piano. I
gave *that* up long ago, but the other day I was alone
for a whole afternoon and I touched the piano
again and played on and on. Four hours later when
people came in I looked at them and couldn't see
them clearly—everything in the room was in vibra-

tion and I felt that I was floating in the air. My eyes were burning, my face was smiling and wouldn't stop; I could only look at the blurred faces around me as if they had no right to speak to me, to recall me from a world they couldn't enter because they had never lived in it. With writing it's the same phenomenon. The slightest interruption, the slightest diversion, makes it impossible to preserve the necessary state. Once you have entered it, and thoughts have begun to find their form, it is agony to be recalled, to be forced back into the broken vibrations of ordinary life; all creation stops, you lose all the thoughts and emotions you would have had. These strangled emotions can never be revived. Once your self-hypnosis has been broken, you can never remember what it was all about.

'It's no use to remind me of Gurdjieff's words, "Once even I was sick man for art". I remember them all too well. I've tried to give up my "states": I've tried, as Orage urged, to "spit out" a book instead of pondering over it. But it doesn't work. Oh, it can be done, but with what result? Such a book will be a failure; mediocre like thousands of others that command no art *attention* because they have been written with no art *intention*.

'All right, I can say, then don't write books. But that's the only kind of work I know how to do. If you're a person with a business job, if you have a career or profession, Gurdjieff doesn't say "Give up your job". On the contrary he says, "Do your job, but give my work first place". Well, I can't. If Gurdjieff's work is to take first place in my life, all the rest will have to be given up; it can't be accomplished in second place, it will have no quality.'

I was talking so fast and so fiercely that I didn't stop to gauge my listener's attitude. 'I can tell you just how it is, how these states happen. . . . I remember a late afternoon in Le Cannet when I was listening to the radio. Flagstaad was singing "Un Rêve" (Grieg, I think), and as I listened I was looking out the window at an olive tree. Its leaves were barely stirring in the still air. "They're not silver", I said to myself as the song went on; "they're white-gold like my bracelets" . . . and at once I was in a state of dream that matched Grieg's dream. The spell continued long after the song ended, and before night came I had begun my new book.

'You see,' I finished, 'you must give your life to a book—before, during, and after its writing, through all its revisions. If I must give up my self-induced moods I will have nothing to write about, I'll lose all the thoughts and feelings that make a good book.'

When I stopped there was a long pause.

Then I heard her say, 'Margaret, you exaggerate.'

Suddenly I was as quiet as she was. Then I thought, 'Perhaps I do'.

She said, 'Why do you want to have thoughts and feelings like everyone else's? I wait for the time when what you say to me will be different from what everyone says to me—authentic—your own.'

This so startled and incensed me that I had no breath to answer. A new anger seized me. 'But I'm *not* saying what everyone else says,' I raged to myself. 'What I'm saying *is* authentic, and it's interesting. I've always had high standards of interest, and I *know* that most of the people who talk to you couldn't write a good book to save their lives.'

Like a drowning man I watched a reel of my ideas unrolling before my eyes. I seemed to have hours before me in which to say all I wanted to say; but I said it silently to myself, as one talks to one's self in fever.

'How can you imagine that the state of art can be created out of a divided energy? that you can give your total strength to Gurdjieff's work and make a book out of what's left over? How easily do you think a writer comes upon thoughts and emotions in *form*, and therefore worth recording? Don't you remember Orage's words?: "Merely to convey thought is not an art but a craft, if not a trade. Over and above the desire to communicate thought, there is for the artist as writer the desire to make it

prevail in the minds of others; in short, art is a
means of power. To express himself is not enough:
he wishes to impress himself. Readers feel towards
him the repulsion as well as the attraction of the
snake for the bird. Power they instinctively feel is
there, and they are afraid of it. Style is only the
device adopted by great writers to make their
power more attractive. Style is power made gra-
cious. We must write as if Homer and Demos-
thenes were to be our judges, as if our lives depended upon their approval. . . . All perfection is
the fruit of sacrifice. Art is perfect when it seems to
be nature".

'Do you think Orage "spit out" that passage? Of
course not. Such things can't be done. The sacrifice
demanded is the sacrifice of other activities. Think
of Proust! What a good thing that he was ill and
had to shut himself up in a padded room! And
think of the scientist who, when told he was going
blind, said, "Alors, j'aurai moins de distractions".'

But of all these violent musings I said not a word.

Instead, as they raced through my mind, I was
conscious that other thoughts were accompanying
them, and they in turn made me suspect that I was
discussing the wrong subject-matter. Simultaneously I was saying, 'What does all this matter to
the silent person I'm talking to? As she listens she
has been thinking of something else, something

important for me and for all the others who talk to her. All this time she has been preoccupied with a question: "Will this gesticulating person beside me never stop suffering in vain and begin, before it is too late, to become what she might become? Or will she go on merely writing interesting books and listening to beautiful music? Surely she will soon come to know that that isn't enough".'

I don't know how long we sat in silence, or how long I had been imagining what she was thinking, but at last I said, 'I realize that what I've been describing is a state of frenzy, as Pythagoras said; and as Gurdjieff taught: to make art is to use that "finer energy" that should be used for development.'

Still she waited. So I went on.

'I realize that I must now do something else, that something else I've been working at for so many years without understanding how to live it.'

She smiled at me.

'I will try,' I said, 'I will do whatever you say.'

During the long summer that followed this conversation I was given special work to do—simple, very difficult, or not-too-difficult exercises, repeated over and over and, at intervals, changed. I began like a child who has blindly accepted a task.

'But how will I know when I have accomplished

something?' I asked Jeanne de Salzmann.

'I can only tell you', she said, 'that you will *know*.'

This time I had no rebellion against a phrase which, in its words, said nothing. I believed that if I continued to work as I was told to I would come upon that certain, and different, knowing.

During these months I thought a great deal about Gurdjieff's teaching regarding man's suggestibility, his self-hypnotization. And one morning I wakened as if I had lived a long lifetime in the night. I was saying, 'I am de-hypnotized, I may not have to "lose myself" all the time now, I believe I am really de-hypnotized.' And another night, after reading again all the old wonderful abstractions, I was unable to sleep, so deep was my realization that they now meant less to me than before. I had considered them my special portfolio—my only possible relation, I thought, to the Gurdjieff super-knowledge. Now I realized that the kind of knowledge Gurdjieff had tried to teach me was the kind of realization I had just had: the emptiness of words and ideas until they have been incorporated into a process—knowledge turned into being. I thought, 'Perhaps I have finished for ever with my need to feed on purely mental food.'

These experiences—these moments of perception —seemed to me authentic. My new vision of myself was that my former life of ardour and frenzy was something made of paper. And soon I noticed that I was listening to music quite differently, always conscious that I wasn't completely lost in it, and that I didn't need to listen to it all the time. Surely this, I said, is part of that process by which, according to Gurdjieff, we gradually emerge from the self-hypnosis under which we all live.

I told these things to my patient listener.

'Yes,' she said, 'perhaps they are authentic experiences.'

But that was all she would say.

And then one morning I had that flashing vision of the life of the 'soul', which I described earlier.

Again I sought out Jeanne de Salzmann.

'This, then, is the process which is higher than "taking thought"? This is what you meant when you said "You will *know*"? Am I right?'

'Yes,' she answered, 'this shows a growth in your understanding. What you have seen is absolutely right. This is inner vision, truth. This is "to see". But be careful. You see at those moments, and something may remain of that understanding. But it will be right only when you "see" it all the time. And *that* will be an impulse not to continue in the same way as until now. It will give you a need to change further, to go further in that achievement'. . . .

205

## XI

# DEATH OF A MAGE

IT WAS in Paris, at the American Hospital—
on October 29, 1949 that death came to
Gurdjieff.

He had intended to sail on the 20th for New
York, where he would spend Christmas, and we
were going on the same boat; but he became ill
and had to postpone his trip. Instead of changing
to a later sailing, we were advised to go on ahead
and be in New York to welcome him.

We arrived on the 27th. Two days later Solita,
who had stayed on in Paris, cabled:

'Gurdjieff died this morning'.

A few days later her letter came:

*October 30—Sunday midnight.* We are all nearly in despair. Yesterday and today (my birthday) and the days to
come are the worst in my life.

He's wearing his best suit, bought for the American trip. He is lying on a divan, covered to the throat with a pale *coverture* which is piled with red roses, pink orchids, white flowers; on either side of his head are two enormous bouquets of violets. The chapel is lighted with candles.

His face is like a statue's. Yesterday he looked alive still, a slight smile made him seem so; his skin had a most curious lavender tinge. Today he is darker, the smile has gone, he's already far away, the eyes have begun to sink, the lips are in a grave line, though not quite stern. Perhaps it was the taking of the death mask that changed him, but I think not. He looks as if he had just said. 'Now I go away with all my secrets and my mystery. My work is finished here.'

All day for two days and all night last night and still tonight, the people stream to the hospital, stand in line to go in and see him. They stand in the most complete silence I have ever known and just stare at him. Nearly all are crying.

He died at half past ten in the morning yesterday; I had been telephoning for his news at ten and was told that he was the same. I was in the hotel yesterday when R. rang up to say he was dead. As soon as I could move I went to Neuilly, and was told that we could see him as soon as he had been taken to the chapel. Although he had seemed to be sleeping for hours before he died, the doctor had raised his eyelids and had said that Gurdjieff looked back at him and was conscious. A most curious phenomenon: four hours after his death his forehead and

neck were still very warm; the doctor said he couldn't
understand it.

On Friday Mme de Salzmann had spoken to him in
Russian. He did not reply but lifted his hand and held it
out for her to take. She has been absolutely superb. At
the service yesterday she sat near his head with white
face, closed eyes from which the tears slowly flowed.
Today at the service: a Russian intones the prayers, his
assistant sings the responses, we all hold a lighted taper
in our right hands and just gaze and gaze. The chapel is
too small to hold all the people; we crowd together to
make room until we are touching the funeral couch.
Those who cannot enter stand outside and listen. Then
when the service is finished and we go out, the crowds
who are waiting pass in. Of course he is never alone,
several people volunteer each night to watch. On Wednesday he will be taken to the Russian church and at
eleven on Thursday will be the high requiem mass. At
twelve we all go to Fontainebleau for the *enterrement*. In
the meantime there will be a mass every afternoon, for
the people who heard late of his death, especially for the
English who will come.

I think he would be proud of the behaviour of all his
people. The grief is terrible, silent, and has a really objective quality of dignity. Of my own grief I will not
speak; it is a small part of the common catastrophe. I
shall always be grateful to those powers that allowed me
to be here to see him before he went away from the
planet earth. But I shall never be able to describe the
noble beauty of his dead face.

# Death of a Mage

*November 2, midnight.* This is Thursday and at six o'clock we left him six feet deep in the cold ground at sunset, the coffin still uncovered; the last of him I saw, and it was not he, was a long pale brown box, with a golden cross at the head, a few roses some desperate person had thrown in with the handfuls of earth each of the hundreds had dropped, in accordance with the Russian custom.

But back to Monday, at the chapel of the American Hospital. He had turned to grey stone and looked even more 'at peace'.

Jane's English group had arrived in the night, direct from the *gare*. At four a.m. the French group took over. Streams of people came and went all night, as they did all day. I can't imagine what the American Hospital thought of all this, the hundreds of pilgrims who came and went away, all through the icy, frosty night.

*Tuesday.* I'm just back from the chapel. I sat by his side, near his face, for two hours. A small choir came from the Russian church and sang the responses. The chief priest in the old tradition—robe, silver cross and a chain, long black hair and beard, liquid black eyes and honey voice. There were new flowers over the tilleul-silk brocade. Someone had made a tiny bouquet of red roses and late yellow daisies. Gurdjieff's face today was greyer and the skin is tighter over the immense intelligence of his skull.

*Wednesday. Un froid de loup.* Oh, never to see that smile again, never to hear him say—well, no matter what

# Death of a Mage

... *The mise en bière.* I couldn't quite go to the hospital to see him put into the box, and as I found out later, I wouldn't have been allowed to—only the men of the family. I went to the Russian church at four and waited there till nearly six before he was brought. Six men carried him in. Dim lovely lights, many flowers which had arrived early, vested priests and small choir for the services. The church was crowded even for that small ceremony, all golden under the incense-smoke dome. The catafalque was covered with a large black cloth, embroidered with silver. Not a sound ever issues from any gathering of his people—neither a footstep, a cough, a rustle or a breath. A remarkable quality of silence which is so rare as to be noted as unique. (Don't believe in those 'last words' records, as no one thought he would die until he was so weak that he never spoke again, only held out his hand.)

*Last day.* This morning at eleven-thirty the high mass at the Russian cathedral. There had been no *veille* permitted last night, so he had been alone until the church opened. Candles, flowers, the voices of five white-and-gold robed priests, a cantor with a divine breaking voice. How beautiful is the Russian language! The church was packed—not only with those we know, but by hundreds of his followers whom we never saw, whom I had never seen in all my years near him. After the chanting and prayers and singing were finished, for an hour everyone passed by his coffin, one by one, from the right. Each mourner, streaming with tears, made a genuflection at his head, stepped up to the icon at his feet, kissed it, and walked to the left. Each, un-self-conscious, took his or her private and sorrowful farewell to him with a ceremonious simplicity that tore one's heart open even wider than before, if possible. Then everyone went away to breathe, have a drink of coffee, and at two o'clock we came back to the church.

The crowds stood along the street to watch him brought out and put in the great funeral carriage, his flowers placed on top. The family rode with him. The hundreds of others rode behind in the cortège in many private cars and four enormous autobuses. The streets were jammed, closed to traffic for blocks around the Russian church, and other crowds gathered to watch the spectacle. I went with some of the rich silent English, old followers of Ouspensky's. Through the old familiar roads, streets, towns, turnings, forest, to Avon. . . . In a cruel icy sunny wind we walked by the hundreds through the cemetery gates, following him to the family plot. I saw the grave torn open in the rocky watery ground, deep, deep, horribly deep. . . . The porters let him down into it. A great sigh came from the people— the only sound they had made, when they were together, since he died. The priest came to the rescue with his chanting. Later everyone passed by the terrible hole, cast a pinch of earth down on to the box, knelt, made the sign of the cross, and passed on. It was over. He had disappeared from us for ever.

*Later.* Two days before he was taken to the hospital he called in four people who happened to be sitting in the salon through the night and just looked at them for a long time, saying not one word. They believe he was saying good-bye.

The priest at the Russian church stated that there has never been such a funeral before, except Chaliapin's; that he has never seen such mass grief, or such a concentration of attitude on the part of the mourners. Even the undertaker who had never seen Gurdjieff before he saw him dead, broke down at the grave and wept. Just from the vibrations, I daresay.

The French group is going to keep the apartment as a sort of shrine to which we may all go. The group-dances and readings are continuing. Jeanne de Salzmann goes to America in December. She will carry on his work as best she can, and I suppose we will all help her.

We have all so pledged. . . .